for Wilma "*soeur-ma*" surfing our city's waves

Evanescent Isles
from my city-village

Xu Xi

香港大學出版社
HONG KONG UNIVERSITY PRESS

Hong Kong University Press
14/F Hing Wai Centre
7 Tin Wan Praya Road
Aberdeen
Hong Kong

© Xu Xi (a.k.a. S. Komala), 2008 www.xuxiwriter.com

ISBN 978-962-209-946-3

Secure On-line Ordering
http://www.hkupress.org

British Library Cataloguing-in-Publication Data
A catalogue record for this book is available from the British Library.

Printed and bound by Condor Production Co. Ltd., in Hong Kong, China

contents

acknowledgements

Thanks are owed to many who have fed my thinking about my city, and really, I should thank everyone I know in Hong Kong, as well as those I do not personally know, but have heard or read about, listened to on television or radio, or whose words were read, photos or art admired, music heard, performances witnessed, or whose courage inspired. However, for this book, a specific acknowledgement is owed to the following relatives, friends, acquaintances and strangers for, variously, their friendship, time, creative and intellectual inspiration, attachment to this city, attitude, persistence, and admirable bloody-mindedness.

Kingsley Bolton, Tony and Rosalie Carpio, Cheung Kar-ning, Martha P.Y. Cheung, Greg Chako, Hugh Chiverton, Ray Cordeiro, David Clarke, Cliff Deeds, Stacilee Ford, Helen and Lawrence Gray, Mike Ingham, Khouw Boen Lin and family, Agnes S.L. Lam, Lau Kin-wai, "Long Hair" Leung Kwok-hung, "Ya Se" Leung Ping-kwan, Mrs. Christine Liao, Ted Lo, Christine Loh, Daisy Moh, Skip Moy, Raymond Ng, Rebecca Ng, Rita Tung, Susan Reingold, Keith H. Sillett, Nury Vittachi, Jenny Wai, Diane Wilcoxson, Abbe Wong Mee-chun, Allen Youngblood.

And in memoriam, Mohan Mirchandani.

A note of appreciation to the Hong Kong Film Archives in Sai Wan Ho where I was able to spend many hours viewing the work of our independent filmmakers, many of whose films are often sadly unavailable once past the release date.

Special thanks to David Clarke, who kindly allowed use of his photographs, and to William McGuire for his graphic design contribution to the cover.

An excerpt of an earlier version of "A Short History of Our Shores" appeared in *Divide*, University of Colorado, Boulder, Fall 2005 (Arts & Politics issue); an earlier version of "Godspeed" appeared in the inaugural issue of *Saranac Review*, State University of New York, Plattsburgh, Fall 2005; "Pop Goes the Idol" appeared in a shorter version as "Hung Your Heads" in the *South China Morning Post*, February 20, 2005.

a crack in space

because we must begin somewhere . . .

Visitors in my city hear this announcement: "Please mind the gap between the train and the platform." The tone is feminine and formal; the accent surfs the waves of English that is the Queen's, American-global and Canto-local. It cautions riders of the MTR — the people's name for the Mass Transit Railway, our metro, subway, tube, underground — as you pull into each station. What fewer visitors comprehend is the preceding Cantonese announcement: 請小心列車與月台間之空隙 *"Please have a little heart for the crack in space from the train to the platform," which is a creative, but not entirely unrecognizable, translation.*

Hong Kong occupies a tiny crack in the space of world history. We were that "barren isle," sacrificed by China and disdained by England, but we flourished, like some unstoppable weed in our "borrowed" space and time. In 1939, the poet W.H. Auden observed of the city: *Here in the East the bankers have erected / A worthy temple to the Comic Muse.* Now that his century is past, it is perhaps time to reflect on the worth of that temple, this place I'll call home for as long as it makes me laugh and sing and feel.

We have become a cosmopolitan people, though still undeniably a brand of Chinese, who trade in the languages and commodities of the world. To be a "Hong Kong citizen" allows you to absorb the best of east and more east, and to know the nuance of west vs. east if you choose. Do the twain really meet? Occasionally yes, but perhaps more often, no. Our children marry across races and produce offspring of multiple hues who are not "lost in translation," unlike cosmopolitans from the West. Yet you will find Chinese traditions and attitudes, dating back hundreds of years, nascent in this post-post-modern space. Our public holidays and festivals cling to old myths and superstitions long abandoned in modern China. We like to insist our contemporary culture is less global-Western-ized, democratic, and confused than it really is.

In 1997, Hong Kong was returned to the People's Republic. It was our great historical moment of controversy. The moment was dubbed the handover, or takeover — some might say the homecoming — and rattled no one who truly knew the city. The international media took a different view, sounding warning bells over the arrival of the PLA (People's Liberation Army). Like all newsworthy moments, this historical hump over which we flew was quickly forgotten as the Asian economic crisis took hold, followed by bird flu, S.A.R.S., and saber-rattling by Beijing over Taiwan, that other Chinese political anomaly. We blip across the news, as protestors march for democracy backed by international political support. The support is, however, neither resounding nor heeded by Beijing. At this moment, we are pushing limits on "universal suffrage" in this non-nation state that has never been a democracy. In the game of diplomatic relations, you've got to, as the song goes *win a little, lose a little / yes, and always have the blues a little* and, at least in our times, trust that the glory of capital markets, like love, will prevail. "The Glory of Love" (1939) was used as the theme song of a 1967 film, *Guess Who's Coming to Dinner,* once controversial for its interracial subject matter. Controversy is like that, good for the moment. We pretend lessons are learned, but then move on, soldier on we might say, while few things change to still our little hearts.

So *siu sam,* or have a "little heart," which is to say, be wary of that crack in space. It might trip you up with its transformation now that we are once again more or less on our own, the way we were when a handful of fisher folk and farmers roamed these shores, more or less governed by China. We never were "British" just as most of us are not "Chinese" the way they are on the Mainland. But just as we once became, if not a little more British then at least a little more international, we can now become a little more Chinese the way they are up north. We are a gambling culture after all. *Crack or platform, platform or crack.* Like the Macau casino "Big-Small" game that pays two to one, a fifty-fifty chance might be the odds on our space in eternity.

While reflecting on the "crack," I began wandering through my life in this, my birth city. It seemed at first an aimless journey through memory, supplemented by present-day conversations about Hong Kong, provoked by the stimuli offered in the city's writing, art, performances, photography, films, as well as by the minutiae of day-to-day living. During the decade since the handover, I have flitted in and out of this place, sometimes alighting for six weeks or longer, at other times zipping through for a fortnight or less on my way elsewhere. As of mid 2006, I have returned for family reasons to live on a more-or-less temporary, medium-term basis, a state of being which might speak to the true nature of this place.

Yet what began to emerge, as I poked my way through remembrances, was a narrative thread — a Jamesian *ficelle* — that pulled me along actual streets and districts on long, uncertain walks, and rides on public transport, at all hours of the night and day. Sometimes, these journeys had a destination: to see a forgotten locale, to discover a new and unknown area, to visit a friend, to go to a club or restaurant, to swim or run, to research a detail for fiction. More often than not, I perched in tea shops, restaurants, bars, or cafés that I stumbled upon, trying to come to grips with what was happening to my city, measuring my life here in numerous bowls of noodles and congee, cups of coffee and tea, glasses of wine and other spirits, knowing that T.S. Eliot's coffee spoons could not, would not, should not suffice. Similarly, I obsessively eavesdropped conversations on board buses, trams, minibuses, and in the carriages of the MTR and KCR (the Kowloon Canton Railway). *Where have you come from, where are you going to,* I wanted to ask strangers, as if their answers could reveal the meaning of these isles — located in the Landrone chain of the South China Seas — as well as the identity of a people who are not easily classified as "Chinese," despite the ethnicity of the overwhelming majority.

To write of this city is to be thwarted at every turn. My stories needed to tell more than show — a deadly problem for fiction as any storyteller knows — and words tumbled out in a new and different form, in essays rather than fiction, to tell, tell, tell of the *crisis of calm* that holds my city in thrall. But at heart I am neither a critic nor journalist nor academic — even though to earn a living I have occasionally pretended to be all three — and cannot write of life primarily by those terms of engagement. I am a writer of fiction, and it became my challenge to find a creative voice in non-fiction to articulate the intersection of memory and moment as it worried the imagination.

It has not been easy coming to terms with being a writer from these shores. As a child, I awoke at four one morning and began to write after gazing at the Hong Kong harbor. Then, scribbling in a notebook was simply another life activity, not unlike sleeping or playing or going to school, except that it proved more fun. Yet now when my identity is inextricably tied to "being a writer," I question the scribbling of personal narratives and essays of this place and people, even though I count myself a Hong Kong person. The density is daunting. There are too many lives, loves, sorrows, celebrations, emotions, experiences. Too many stories. As fast as I tell one, the next awaits, demanding its turn. The spatial challenge is, at times, unbearable. The shifting shapes of buildings and boundaries are like the vanishings in a ghostly flick, designed to frighten and thrill. The lights go on, though, at the end of a film, and you file out of the cinema, impressed, disappointed or merely indifferent. In the real world, the map is less certain. Finding your way can be a stumble down a blind alley, the pursuit of an unfinished path or arrival at, as the old song goes, *number 54 / the house with a bamboo door / bamboo roof and bamboo walls / it's even got a bamboo floor,* where, if you surrender to the controlled chaos within, you'll find out "why there's a lot to do" in this strange and sometimes unreal space.

As a fiction writer, I am generally discomfited by memoir, because few lives strike me as necessary to record in this form, least of all mine. The "I" must mean more than merely "me, me, me," otherwise such words deserve less attention than the millionth of a second reality TV deserves. In trying to shape this book, it was not an "I" but a "we" that emerged, because the life of my city mattered more than my own. Was Hong Kong itself asking for attention? It appeared so, because the city that once seemed solid and real was dissolving, transforming (some would say disappearing) but nonetheless surviving (many would say thriving), stoic and undeterred, while doggedly ignoring the protests, complaints and demands of voices who sense a threat to their survival or who deem survival alone insufficient.

We are a peace-loving, law-abiding, hard-working, generally apolitical people, more given to shopping than shouting, more consumed by frenzy than reflection. Why then a *crisis* of calm, this apparent oxymoron? A climactic calm is characterized by an absence of wind and freedom from storms, high winds or rough activity. Our city's storms, whether economic, viral or social, have hit squally seas slightly larger than teacups, quickly followed by periods of calm. The etymology of calm is curiously contradictory, because its Greek and Latin roots are heat, burning heat, and even, to burn.

Is it a crisis, then, this stillness that burns the heart? Crisis is a turning point — its linguistic root being to separate — as well as an unstable state, usually political, economic or psychological. If Webster's is to be trusted, then to define such instability is especially true for "a social condition requiring the transformation of existing cultural patterns and values." Hence this crisis of calm, as we watch the changeover from extant to new that is different, perhaps, but not entirely unrecognizable.

As I write this, when I am not yet quite 54 — the number on that bamboo door — but shall be by the time keystrokes on a screen transform into a book, tangible, which will be, if I do my job right, readable, what remains is to offer these pages to the spirit of Hong Kong. A little then of me, you, us, in these words for the city we cannot help but know, despite whatever may be its future, or as we say in Cantonese, whatever is its "yet to come."

Summer 2007
from a rooftop squat in the shadow of Lion Rock

cracks in space of an over-privileged childhood

life in the city, the orient's pearl . . .

GLORIES OF THE NOUVEAU RICHE

Oh to be young again! And just foreign and *nouveau riche* enough to glory in Hong Kong of the early sixties.

Ours was a lucky family. Dad bragged to relatives about the money he earned and acquired multiple symbols of this new found wealth: an Italian chandelier, oddly bright in our tiny living room and excruciatingly difficult to clean; the custom-made, showcase, fully-stocked bar, triangular-shaped to fit under the staircase of our harbor-view, penthouse duplex; a white, handset telephone, its dial on the base with a red, circular switch in the center that clicked off and on; our own hand dryer, installed next to the handwashing basin behind the bar; the made-to-order, midnight-blue, wool carpet, buttoned around the pillar that split our living room — into not half, but an awkward two-thirds — and which covered approximately three quarters of the entire downstairs. The carpet needed to be removed each spring because of the humid, subtropical climate, and was unwieldy, but it was the closest my father could approximate wall-to-wall carpeting, that great foreign luxury.

Meanwhile, Mum was restored to her glory as favorite daughter of one of the formerly richest men in the village of Tjilatjap in Central Java. She installed three live-in servants, ordered blue, pink and yellow wooden beds plus matching wardrobes for her three girls, bribed the Catholic priests and nuns with donations to ensure all the children's attendance at the elite, English-medium "name schools," enrolled us for piano, ballet, swimming and tennis lessons (but only after we endured Chinese and math tutors), and hosted numerous parties for my father's relatives and business associates. She wore cocktail dresses tailor-made at the Old Peking Silk Store on Nathan Road, and commandeered feasts: caviar and champagne; Chinese hot-pot or sukiyaki with hot *sake,* replenished repeatedly by the cook; cheese fondue to accompany Japanese greenhouse strawberries that came packed in straw in small wooden crates. On the verandah overlooking a harbor where Chinese junks sailed and U.S. aircraft carriers docked, we charcoal grilled beef-chicken-pork-goat *satay,* or steaks to be served on individual wooden boards, because to eat rich is to be glorious, even before Deng Xiaoping.

In our post-handover city, my childhood is no longer as exotic as it once seemed. I recognize huge shards of that life among the globalized citizen-children whose parents pay exorbitant fees for their attendance at "international" schools, who fly business class to Switzerland or Bali or Los Angeles for Christmas break, who swarm the Sunday buffets at five-star hotels and routinely dine on oysters, sushi, *fromage*, select steaks from Argentina, Colorado or Australia, specify wines from Chile, New Zealand and of course France, gulp cognac by the thousands of gallons. Interior designers do a flourishing trade and, I daresay, a better job at glamorizing home space than my father once did.

To be rich is relative in a capitalist paradise, but the memory of that early wealth lingers when I consider my changing city. My lucky family lost that wealth by the time I was eleven, although given Chinese glue that holds "face" in place, it was difficult for outsiders to tell. But my number two sister and I, as the oldest children, were keenly aware that something was seriously awry when Mum emptied our bank accounts of our carefully hoarded *laisee* earnings, when Dad stayed home more and more often and swept the floor after the last maid was let go, when my parents stopped traveling and never went home to Indonesia, or anywhere else, to visit family.

Eventually, my mother went back to work as a pharmacist. This was the woman who once pitied the wives of friends who "had to work" since her view of a woman's education was that it should provide earning power only until marriage, or if your husband couldn't support you. Wealth is fickle, more so than woman; my father's fondness for opera ensures that *La Donna è Mobile* replays in my head, an irritating soundtrack to life.

I remember falling into that crack in space. At the time, it was simply life, and frankly, did not seem all that strange or terrible. But the cracks in my parents' lives were harder for them to bear.

My father was the eldest of three sons. Although he never finished university, he encouraged his two brothers onto their PhDs, and helped out financially where he could. When Dad was eighteen his mother passed away. Less than a year later, my grandfather married a woman some thirty years his junior and sired another five children; his wife was my mother's age and their youngest son, my step uncle, is my age. In the sixties, their family lived in Jesselton, since renamed Kota Kinabalu. Two of my step aunts came, in succession, to live with us and attend secondary school in Hong Kong. It was assumed that my successful and wealthy father (he did brag, after all) should easily assist in supporting his step sisters. My mother, being a modern, educated woman when it suited her, was quick to protect her own children's interests, and protested vehemently. The feuds that ensued — between my father and grandfather, my mother and my father's family, my mother and father — on top of the strain of tight finances, became our family's never ending thrum, like a perpetual bad disco beat. *No big deal if we had the money* . . . money became the thing that would make all pain go away.

Ah, illusions and delusions of grandeur! These wafted around my girlhood and the romance of it all was enough to make you giddy. Pretty dresses and birthday cakes and parties made my lucky family special. My childhood girlfriends still recall those parties, in the days when my mother's greatest responsibility was to ensure that all her children gave the most lavish and memorable parties, with more food than anyone could finish and games and prizes for all. Few Chinese friends had parties at home, except for one or two who were truly rich, and not merely *nouveau*.

My father survived life in the cracks by clinging to the joy that money once bought, because he refused to surrender certain extravagances — the cost of an overseas subscription to *Kompas,* the Indonesian newspaper, for instance, probably because it was a reminder of his manganese mining business in Java that had once made him important and rich — and these became the sources of friction between my parents.

It was however harder for Mum, because women get the short end, despite the vote and other liberations. While Dad sank into a silent depression at home, too proud to see people, refusing to take "lesser" work — translations, for example, which he was capable of doing — sometimes not speaking a word for days except to shout at us for making a mess, my mother swallowed pride and borrowed money, sold her jewelry, stretched budgets, bought nothing for herself, and kept a family clad and fed to face the world as if nothing was wrong. Even the most obedient adolescents are difficult, as I was, and her rage found its outlet in recriminations against my father, and in an oftentimes irrational control over the children. If she clung to anything, it was to an inflated sense of superiority. As our family sank into the mire, she constantly judged everyone around us as lesser beings, never as good as we were, and held us up to impossibly high standards without regard for our real abilities or inclinations. It was xenophobic, her diatribes against all our friends and relatives. This vitriol was spewed at home, behind their backs, to stay within our walls. Home was the most dangerous place to be.

It was fear, colored by melodrama, because she perhaps could not see then how we would ever get out, how we would ever find a safe space for ourselves again. By keeping everything difficult, perpetually on edge, we would learn to survive. We the children were doomed to disappoint her, as we all managed to do with alarming efficiency over time.

The largest crack appeared when we moved out of our home. It was my mother's decision, and financially and pragmatically, a sound one for the family. Our penthouse flat in Tsimshatsui was mortgage-free and a good source of rental income. Meanwhile, suburban areas were springing up in Kowloon, and cheap mortgages were available for new developments. The property solution is very Hong Kong, and over my father's objections, my mother found a new flat, organized the purchase, and arranged to move away from the harbor and our semi-commercial building into a smaller, top-floor, residential space with roof rights on Beacon Hill Road. This was nearer to all our schools, and as far away as possible from the pride of Dad's glory days.

The balance of power had shifted completely. It was unnerving.

This move took place during my School Certificate year which was sufficiently pressure-filled, but I was spared some of the agony because Mum sent me to live with my maiden aunts so that I could study hard, ace the exams and get a scholarship for university. Suffice to say that I eventually went to university on a wing and a loan from my schoolteacher aunt, to major in English no less. It was my truly smart cousins who got academic scholarships to Ivy Leagues because they, unlike me, really could ace exams, while I just got by. My mother never got the doctor she wanted, as I was the only one out of all my siblings who might have done so (although by thirteen, I knew better). I barely passed biology, chemistry, physics and failed calculus miserably.

When I escaped family life at seventeen, I never wanted to go home again.

In 1998, my father died abruptly and unexpectedly, but peacefully, in bed one night, at the age of seventy-five, the result of an undetected abdominal aneurysm. He never again was as rich as he had been in the sixties, but he had by then semi-reconciled himself to a more modest, albeit comfortable life. The harbor-view, penthouse duplex, the home he so prized, was long sold. He and my mother had fostered a longstanding truce that, in celebratory moments, could still seem like a kind of love. My grandfather outlived him, although he no longer remembered much, and died a few years later shortly after turning one hundred. A very switched-on Hong Kong lady told me that my father gave me a "good fortune" with that death, meaning that he did not burden us with having to care for him. I was struck by her observation because I realized that despite the grief that initially overwhelmed me, it was possible to make peace with his passing.

The shock to my mother was profound, and I am not sure she will ever entirely recover. Suddenly, she had no one to complain about and, more important, she no longer had anyone to look after, because she did care for him all those years despite the fissures in their marriage. A couple of years afterwards, Mum was diagnosed with Alzheimer's, and we four siblings must deal with the difficulties of that form of aging, where memory is completely defunct at one moment about a meal eaten five minutes earlier, and startlingly exact at another about a long-forgotten hurt of the remote and distant past.

Today, as I ponder my "home" city which has seen many cycles of bust and boom, cycles that seem to be characteristic of its nature if not its soul, I wonder about the essence of my family as it once was compared to what it has become. Former residents sometimes say that they cannot recognize Hong Kong, that it has changed too dramatically. All places change, but our particular slice of paradise seems to loom unusually large for many who have once known this place as home. We seem to desire connection, the way some people do, even to their devastatingly bad families. We nurse nostalgia in our films and songs. We take such pride in our way of life even as we reconcile our existence with other ways of being. Colonial, Communist, International, Chinese. It's all Hong Kong because we seem to know that the balance of power is always precarious, will always shift, sometimes this way, sometimes that, and survival depends on keeping our balance in that tiny crack in space.

I have spent my life building and dismantling homes, perching here, there and everywhere, returning to my city because the pull seems inescapable. My over-privileged childhood is just as inescapable. It was this place that made such a childhood possible, that made me what I was and have become.

In my mother's home now, as her memory and spirit fade despite a healthy constitution, Dad's Italian chandelier still hangs, not unlike those in countless other *nouveau riche* Hong Kong homes today that lust after a past era of European elegance. My father's *lumière* is a burst of cylindrical tubes, petals of a crystal chrysanthemum. The entire fixture must be taken down, each tube carefully cleaned by hand, if it is to sparkle brilliantly, the way it once did, illuminating our lost harbor view. My number two sister was the last person to take on this task, which she did with the kind of care and precision that would have made Dad proud, while Mum fretted, the way she would at any disturbances to our father's treasures. The chandelier is an awkward thing, too large and grand for the modern room. My mother rarely turns it on, preferring to use a cheap, clip-on light behind her armchair.

But occasionally, one of us will flip the switch, and light floods the space. All the pragmatic, ordinary things of daily living fade out and surrender to this extravagant spotlight. Perhaps we need this glare from time to time, to remind us of what was as we wander forward, because we must, along this mysterious path of becoming.

GODSPEED

The day our cook threatened to quit, I witnessed my first layoff.

The victim was Ah Siu. Hers was a no-name name, without clear demarcation for a family or first name. Back when my father still had money in the sixties, she was hired to look after the four children. "Nanny" would be too classy, "domestic helper" too modern and politically correct. Back then she was a "servant," along with our cook and washerwoman.

When she first arrived, I was around nine and promptly fell in love. She was everything my mother could not be: lenient, undemanding, tolerant of my childishness. Most of all, she seemed to favor me, or so I imagined, the unworthy eldest child whose only job in the family was to serve as an "example" for the younger ones. I despised my exemplary role, even as I guarded it with fierce pride, relishing the privilege of being told that *Mummy must take care of brother because he's sickly, or sister who's still small, or sister who's not as good a girl as you.* I didn't always trust that praise, wondering if perhaps Mummy actually didn't want to take care of me. Ah Siu gave me all her time, listening to my stories, paying me undivided attention, treating me like her own girl.

All three servants boarded with us, sharing a bedroom in the rear two-bedroom guest flat we owned, and only had one day off. They were expected to start work at sunrise and retire at night, often quite late. My parents did not like us spending time in their quarters, but I hung out in the rear apartment, curious and lovestruck, my excuse being the piano which I practiced in that living room. I thought of the servants as part of our family because, despite everything my parents said to the contrary, I saw no difference between them and us, especially not Ah Siu.

It was a shock, then, when she told me she had a home in the New Territories and a little girl, a daughter she saw once a week, on Sundays, her day off. How could she belong to someone else? She was my Ah Siu, mine! Yet I quickly swallowed that thought, overwhelmed instead with sorrow that Ah Siu couldn't live with her family, and turned my anger towards my parents, Mum especially, that such employment injustice existed. However, this did not translate into *my* not having Ah Siu. I was a pragmatic, if melodramatic child.

After that, I treated Ah Siu with a little distance, except when the desire to be babied overwhelmed. If my report card was less than stellar, Ah Siu gave me a never-mind smile. If Ah Yee, the cook, yelled, as she often did, I could flee to Ah Siu's tenderness. I was not a sissy child, and in fact, resisted tears to win the "good girl" accolade from Mum. But what I recall of Ah Siu was a sweet refuge in the raucous household of my childhood, where my father was often overseas on business, my mother overwhelmed and exhausted by the household and servants, where guests needed "to be waited on hand and foot" as Mum said of our numerous Indonesian relations, especially those of my father's, because the servants and my mother had to work twice as hard for these folks, accustomed as they were to legions of servants in their large Indonesian homes, in contrast to our puny three.

Then came the big fight, the details of which I never knew, between Ah Yee and Ah Siu. Shouts and tears. Mum intervening. Loud threats by our cook that she would quit, right now, if Mum didn't fire *that woman*. Before I knew it, Mum said Ah Siu was leaving. Not a single objection I raised was heard; a good cook, however temperamental, was harder to find.

Ah Siu packed her things and prepared to leave.

I sulked. I refused to leave my bedroom. So what, I told myself, *she's only a servant,* echoing my mother's words.

At the last possible moment, I snatched my favorite thing of the time — a tiny statue of Mercury with his quicksilver wings — and ran to the front door. *Here,* I said, *this is for you,* and tried to tell her about the Greek messenger god. But I was inarticulate, unable to tell a story, unable to arrive at catharsis.

She took the statue, smiled a never-mind smile, hugged me, and we cried in each other's arms.

And now I am grown up, or at least pretend to be, and to date have not perpetuated the indentured servitude of a "domestic helper" for myself. Once, back in the eighties in New York City, I hired a part-time cleaning woman from Columbia. Watching her work, I felt slightly ashamed, because after all I should be capable of cleaning up my own mess. Throughout my adult life in Hong Kong, I have cleaned and cooked for myself. Of course, unlike many friends and acquaintances, I do not have children as well as a career, so I don't have to balance that equation. Yet I cannot help feeling there is something wrong with the equation, that it is fundamentally unsound, even if it is the basis of the global economy of the servant class.

Why is it Hong Kong's well-being depends on perpetuating the servant class?

Today's Ah Siu's are Filipino. Her day off is usually Sunday, and in some households, she works the long, absurd hours of my family's servants back in the sixties. I know all the arguments: Hong Kong provides employment for a nation of people whose economy needs help; our city has laws and does not tolerate abuse or unfair treatment of the servant class; this is just the way of the world, isn't it, that some rule and others serve? The subtext is clear: in the end, they are "only servants," democracy be damned.

Yet what is it about our culture that this upstairs-downstairs practice thrives so long and well, this wholly intolerable thing?

This year, my sister and I became employers, for the first time in both our lives, of two domestic helpers from the Philippines. They do not clean, cook or care for either of our households, because their jobs are to live with and look after our elderly mother who has Alzheimer's, and who needs round-the-clock monitoring. One woman is a qualified nurse, the other an excellent cook. Both of them are educated and intelligent professionals, as well as wives and mothers, hardly "servants." We call them employees, and though I live at my mother's address, my space is separate and I clean it myself. The only concession is to have them do my laundry, as there is only one washing machine on location. But the ironing is my job since I am fussy about my clothes. This is not something I need to employ someone to do for me.

For my mother however, as her memory fades, she has her "girls" at home to simulate the noise and chatter of family, since none of her real family live with her. My mother, as she grows more frail slips in and out of the life she once knew, ordering the "servants" around as a salve to pride, even though they know better than to pay attention. It is unenviable, the way we age today.

And I am merely a messenger, the fleet-of-foot god, with the story of a privileged history I cannot revise. All I can do is try to live a life that does not perpetuate the wholly intolerable, to avoid what strikes me as childish practices, the ones my city seems so unable to eliminate.

PATRIOT'S ACT

As a kid growing up in Hong Kong of the sixties, I *desperately* wanted to be American. I begged for hamburgers and Coke, watched American movies, read

Catcher in the Rye and *Huckleberry Finn* with a conviction that insisted *yes,* I too suffered Holden Caufield's angst or needed to escape on a raft down the Mississippi. America was the land of choice and plenty where, because I believed in comic books more than the heritage of the Middle Kingdom, I could learn to draw, become a writer, and transform myself from a ninety-pound weakling into the figure that held up the world. The harbor was my front yard (we lived on the seventeenth floor), and the docked gray battleships offloaded scores of sailors who danced in my imagination like Astaire or Kelly and stared at blushing girl-women until they fell in love. That *real* sailors scoured the waterfront clutching teenage prostitutes, retching and singing into the night, did not completely discolor the dream. I too would one day sail or fly away and outshoot all the men like Annie Oakley.

Now that I'm middle aged, and a sometimes-reluctant American (or "Asian-American" or "Immigrant"), I make my home somewhere between New York and Hong Kong. I have a yard with too much grass because I cannot afford oceanfront. I rarely eat hamburgers or drink Coke. Hollywood often offends my sensibilities. Real American literature, eclipsed by "literature" of supermodels, pop stars, the latest celebrities or "victims" of the newest self-inflicted "disease," does not sufficiently spark the soul of the nation. The shelves of supermarkets and superstores proliferate packaging and use-by waste for overfull landfills. Yet the global dominance that is American capitalism has been, is and continues to be the "shining path" for Hong Kong and much of the rest of the world.

Why didn't I pledge allegiance to Britain, or, more to the point, China, instead?

There were few Americans in my childhood. Although the girls' school I attended, Maryknoll, was run by a Catholic American order, it was a Hong Kong government-subsidized school which kept our fees relatively low. Our curriculum was colonial-British, the medium of instruction English (except for Chinese class), and the school classified "public." It therefore accepted local students, the vast majority being Chinese and not necessarily Catholic. If you were Catholic, as our family was, you might have an in, especially if the right Franciscan priest put in a good word for you, which is how I got into the school (he was a frequent dinner guest in our home). If you were deemed "foreign," as we being Indonesian citizens were, you had the right to enter the English medium schools and not be required to study Chinese unless you chose to do so, unlike the locals. If you were American, however, you enrolled at International which was the only school that taught an American curriculum.

The handful of nuns from the U.S. who were posted to Hong Kong dwindled over the years, in keeping with the general decline worldwide of Catholic novices, and in secondary school, only one or two actually taught us, although the principal back then was always an American nun. Most of our teachers were Chinese and a few, "foreign." An Indian taught Form 5 English, a Trinidadian covered the first three years of French, and a Scotswoman drilled us in third form math and the correct curtsey to make to the Queen. So there were few Americans in my schoolgirl years, despite Maryknoll.

Yet their brand of liberal American-ness left an odd imprint here and there. We were assigned *Catcher in the Rye,* which was not on the Hong Kong public exam syllabus. Our school held a Halloween party in 1967, when Halloween was virtually unheard of in our city although it is vastly popular today, a true victory of global commerce. Some friends and I staged a *Peanuts* play; to this day, my best friend from school and I remain Charlie Brown and Snoopy to each other. And if Maryknoll girls past the age of puberty had a "reputation," it was not for our innocence or demure behavior, although, as everyone knew, it was the students at International who were truly wild.

And so the myth began, of what America was. I never knew an actual student at International back then, but I knew what an American high school ought to be like because of *Archie* and *Superboy* comic books. Perhaps if I had continued to study Chinese, which I dropped after Primary V, I might have been less subject to the influence of other "foreign" students. These were mostly Portuguese, a few Eurasians and Indians, one English and one Danish girl, a Vietnamese and the odd visiting American — she attended our school less than a year — the daughter of someone from the movie set of *The Sand Pebbles,* filmed on our shores.

Yet most of us, local or "foreign," knew little about real Americans other than what our imaginations and popular culture confirmed. My father's business associates were Japanese, English, Indonesian, Shanghainese, Portuguese and later Filipino. These visitors to our home were a great curiosity in my childhood. Their names were exotic: Takeuchi, Halim, Bolingbrook, da Motta, Grosvenor, Baltazar, Huang (with an H, not the run-of-the-mill, local-Cantonese W for Wong). Their accompanying women were equally so: from Wales, that weird and mysterious country, a former Bluebell dancer and soprano whose voice rang through our home in duets with my father; an Englishwoman who was tall and imperious, spoke with all the proper pebbles and served proper teas; the most elegant and refined lady from Tokyo who appeared in a kimono and gazed, not at cherry blossoms, but at the Hong Kong skyline from our flat; the Shanghainese wife and mother who steamed exquisite turnip cake, packed with chives, dried shrimp and sliced sausage, a gift to our family for lunar new year.

One real American did, however, find his way into our home, thanks to Dad.

It was late evening, closer to night, and probably spring or autumn, because it was neither cold enough for wool nor hot enough for air conditioning. The year might have been 1963 or '64 or '65. All I know for sure is that U.S.

battleships were a regular sight in the harbor, and along the waterfront that was part of our neighborhood, life could be rough and the sex trade proliferated.

We four children and Mum had finished dinner when Dad's key clicked in the front door. He was red-faced (*drunk!* my mother later angrily exclaimed) and not alone. With him was a Caucasian American sailor. Although I didn't know a lot about U.S. Naval rankings, I knew enough to tell from his uniform that he wasn't an officer.

"This is _____," said Dad. "He's from _____." Dad went on to say they had met at a bar.

The rest of the family gazed at this being. My father was not in the habit of bringing home complete strangers from bars, although he did occasionally do so. The one other I most recall was an Indonesian sailor who later became a regular visitor. His origins were equally as murky as those of this man who stood before us and said, in that flat, mid-Western accent which is so universally North American, "Hi."

I was astonished. Here was my first real American. He wasn't either handsome or tall, nothing like Cary Grant or Clark Gable or even Kirk Douglas. He wasn't cute, not like some of the fresh-faced sailor boys who swarmed the nights of their R & R. He didn't shake like Elvis or fly like Superman or croon like the Beach Boys. He had no talent to amuse the way Jack Benny or Phil Silvers did. And he didn't talk funny like Bugs or Daffy or Yogi or even Huckleberry Hound. Could this *really* be an American?

In fact, as I studied this person from as polite a distance as possible, who he most reminded me of was Larry from *The Three Stooges*.

The man stayed for a drink and some food, which my mother served, albeit unwillingly. He said he had children about our age and showed us some photos. This is about all I remember of him, because after that night, we never saw or heard from him again. How he piqued my curiosity! I badgered my father with questions about him, but Dad had little to add. Perhaps he had been nothing more than friendly bar chat, although why he intrigued my father enough to invite him home is something I'll never know.

Mum, on the other hand, was livid for days, months, even years afterwards. If my parents fought about this, I did not hear them do so. What I did hear was my mother's telling and re-telling of this incident out of earshot of Dad so that it grew to mythic proportions. *How dare he how could he why did he* gave way soon enough to *What if this man came here one day when Dad was away, then what?!* Over the years, this amalgamated into the threat of potential rape or murder, even of child prostitution (my mother was once approached by a foreign "gentleman" in our building who thought she was the madam of young girls, meaning my sister and I). Her real objection, however, was that Dad had no common sense in trusting this stranger, this American, a member of a race about which we knew nothing at all.

And yet, and yet, I wondered.

One of my mother's favorite TV program was *The Three Stooges,* a show that already bored me by the time I was eight. Its name in Chinese is "Three Stupids" and it was popular in Hong Kong with local audiences because it was broadcast on the Chinese channel. Many American shows limited broadcast to the English channels. Ask any local of my generation or even younger, and chances are, they will know these three Americans, although they might not have heard of Bob Hope. Visual humor translates the way linguistic humor does not, just as an imagined America remains desirable even when the real one offends.

It was Mum, not Dad who really wanted all us children to further our education in the United States. In fact, a few years after this American visitor to our home, when I was around twelve or thirteen, Mum applied for and received a U.S. visa for the family on the strength of her profession as a pharmacist, one that was a high priority for the immigration lottery at the time. That immigrant visa was the highlight of my youthful sense of America. *Maybe Hawaii,* Mum whispered, and my sister and I lusted for Five-O waves, co-ed schools where no one wore uniforms and dates with boys in convertibles. America was this one gigantic space, the Pacific be damned. T-birds, Route 66, Motown, long guitar solos on *Light My Fire,* Aretha Franklin, Hearts in San Francisco, Impossible Missions, Guess Who *Is* Coming to Dinner? For the brief time I thought we really might go West, far West, farther than Chinese Monkey's trip to India, I was ecstatic.

Dad flatly refused. *What will I do in America? Clean their toilets?* And that was that.

So the Stooge look-alike, with his curly hair, squat build and laughing eyes, was the closest I got to America as a child. The real member of the three Stooges, Larry Fine (born Larry Feinberg) was from the south side of Philadelphia and, like my father, played violin. He and his wife Mabel lived in hotels, a permanently transient life which strikes me as romantic and quite un-American, and had two children and five grandchildren.

My family's Larry clone might have been from Sacramento or Dubuque or Rochester for all I know. His children might, if their father told them tales that entranced them, be somewhere in Hong Kong today. I have no idea whether or not he played violin, but if he did, that would have given him and my father something to talk about.

All we humans can do is touch each other a moment and move on, across this strange globe of ours, trusting in dreams and desire, placing faith in the fiction that shapes our lives.

Et Tu Mon Père?

So there I was, fourteen, full of Shakespeare and Dickens and Keats, which was all we knew of English Literature as Form 3 came to an end, although what continued to puzzle me was the coefficient of heat, which I still hadn't conquered in Physics, or the a-b-c of Algebra, which I would not truly comprehend for at least two more years, just in time for School Certificate Math, which got me a pass in the public exam, but only just.

My girlfriends and I were addicted to "personality books," and we assiduously filled in each other's notebooks with data and secrets during, between and after classes. Mine was comprehensive, demanding information worthy of a database long before students used laptops as notebooks or cell phones as ears. Once past the more mundane details (favorite colors, flowers, movies, TV shows, actors, actresses, singers, *et al)* there followed the vital stats (first love, first boyfriend *or* girlfriend — we allowed for lesbian secrets in our all-girls school — first kiss). Vital stats were answered in code for which only your best friend had the key but which everyone else could guess at. "46," a.k.a. "T.R." was my first love, a Eurasian boy from a neighborhood boys' school I had danced with once at a party. 4 letters in his first name, 6 in his last. Such foolish things absorbed our days of hormones and innocence as summer approached, another school year ending. Vacation was time to dream, to write stories for mine eyes alone, to read the optional booklist Mrs. Liao, our English teacher, had given us. I had my public library card and was poised to start with Richardson's *Pamela,* the literary, if dreary, answer to hormones and innocence and the safeguarding of a maiden's virtue, although it was vice, not virtue, that tempted your soul, forcing new definitions of right and wrong. Pamela, I decided that summer, was a fool, and wrong, dead wrong. Her saving grace was to provide the English novel an epistolary form.

The end of Form 3, however, signaled another milestone for your future which, in my mother's eyes, was the all important, only thing that mattered. By some peculiar metaphoric assignation, we were "streamed" into Science, Arts and Domestic Science based on our grades and talents. The syllabus from then on was a tailored cram towards the nine subjects for your School Certificate public exams at the end of Form 5. This sounds democratic enough, but in the Hong Kong school system of the 1960's, and even today, we know democracy is illusory at best. The system was all about class, if not your present social class then undoubtedly your future one, unless of course your family was already rich and would continue to be, in which case, you could fail School Cert and life would still be a hotbed of roses.

If you wanted to go to university, meaning of course, if you wanted a shot at an upper class life, you *had* to get into Science or Arts. Domestic Science girls were curiously self negating: not as clever as *you*, they'd say to those of us whose marks streamed us into the A (Arts) or B (Science) classes in Form 4. In a world of equals, some will always be more equal than others, although even then, I suspected this way of looking at the world was dead wrong. The future vindicated, because plenty of the "not as clever" girls went on to universities, good careers, excellent lives. Even then I knew, life is not only about a 100 in Biology. Personality counted too.

Meanwhile, at home, Vesuvius erupted. *Ma mère* was livid. There I was, fourteen, report card in hand with an average result — great in some subjects, okay in others, not so good in Science and Math, thanks to the exigencies of the coefficient of heat and the x-y-z of Algebra. *This will not do,* she shouted. *You must take Sciences.* How could that be, I wondered, when my A's were in English, Literature, French with respectable B's in History and Religion (a subject I was later to fail). How could that be, I asked myself, when I could perform piano on stage at the Music Festivals each year and score respectable 80+'s, when I danced ballet and passed exams (albeit not well) but could at least recall choreography with ease. Of course, piano and ballet were extracurricular, mere hobbies and not to be taken seriously, I was reminded. To underline the point, ballet lessons ended, not that I minded since I already knew I was no Margaret Fonteyn or even a future *corps de ballet* candidate. But piano, I would not yet surrender my music until Form 5, even though I knew that "pianist" was not a real career option given my limited talent. Limited, yes, but good enough to know that music helped me make sense of the world, and so I hung on as long as possible. Instead I gave up the Legion of Mary which, by that summer, had begun to seem like such unattainable virtue, way beyond the reach of this vice-driven soul.

Meanwhile, Mother. *The nuns are wrong!* The nuns, in my mother's experience, were always wrong, from back in her Singapore school days at the French convent before the war, where girls learned to sew and cook and keep quiet, instead of untangling the coefficient of heat and the parentheses of Algebra, or memorizing the elements table (*hydrogen, helium, beryllium, boron* — wasn't that a petrol brand, boron moron?). My mother is a pharmacist, or was before she married my father, a career hard won in post-war Hong Kong. My mother was an ace Science student at St. Mary's Canossian, and could have gone to the University of Hong Kong to study medicine if not for a lack of funds. My sister and I have more or less confirmed this latter assertion, at least the part about acceptance into the university, in the quest for truth about our muddled family history. But the moment of eruption was not rational or calm or inquiring: there I was, report card in hand, and the future not yet a clearly lighted path. For once, I kept quiet and did not "cross mouths" with Mum, as this verbal delinquent was often wont to do.

Two years later my sister, similarly streamed into Arts, transferred herself out of Maryknoll Convent to Diocesan Girls' School, after cramming all summer to pass an exam that allowed her into Form 4 Sciences, so as not to suffer my fate.

Somewhere in the background, Dad hid. My father rarely interfered in matters of the children's education, except to nod approval when we did not fail outright. Even when we did fail, as we all eventually failed our primary school Cantonese, his response was to surrender and allow us into "study group English" with the non-Chinese crowd, and later, in secondary school, to French. *Dans la rue, il y a un réverbère*, I intoned in Form 1, entranced by the alliteration of "street" and "lamppost" in a foreign tongue, and later, when my sister also knew French, we would cross Cantonese and French with Pig Latin into a parentally undecipherable language, a necessity for teenagers in modern times.

Somewhere in the back of my mind, Dad was the trump card, the safety zone, the space I could retreat to when my mother's Science tirade was over.

Understand, of course, that Mum directed her tirade purposefully. She began, as any good Chinese woman will, with subterfuge and persuasion. Surely my teacher would understand! Mrs. Liao was not moved. My flow into the Arts stream was entirely fair, as my marks proved. The next step was bribery, a longstanding Chinese custom. Flowers for Sister Rose, the principal, and the suggestion, a generous donation to the school, perhaps? Surely this American nun, unlike those French nuns of yore, would see reason, especially since her daughter was destined for great things one day in the United States? Sister Rose was not moved either by the bribe or the force of my mother's presence, although she was willing to entertain a compromise. I had to enter 4A, but if I could catch up to the syllabus on my own in September, she might reconsider.

For my part, I hid at home, horrified.

And so began a long, humid, hellish summer of Science and Math. My bikini hung limp, the piano rarely touched. I did finish *Pamela* and much of Mrs. Liao's list, hoping that this would somehow redeem me come September.

Dog days end, faster than we imagine, and before I knew it, there I was in 4A, together with the smart cousin I worshipped and other friends, with Mrs. Liao as our form mistress. I harbored a secret that no one knew: I would attempt to switch to Science. A month into Form 4, every afternoon had passed with tutors at home, struggling through the Science syllabus, while at school, I absorbed as much of Eliot and Shakespeare and Auden as I could, afraid of the moment when this might end. Science students did not take Literature or Geography to make room for Calculus, with a concession to History. The logic or illogic of our syllabus was not the issue: this was just the way it was.

My mother persisted, nagged. In the end I suspect Sister Rose surrendered, in much the way my family all did in the face of my mother's determination. One day, I walked out of 4A and into 4B, and for the rest of the year, I drew the angle of refraction around blocks of glass, thumbed the four figure table to defeat Trigonometric equations, and told myself, *this is right, this is smart, this is the thing to do* even as I stared, terrified, at the zero on Algebra and other quizzes, and the just-barely-passes in Chemistry. The terror has long been laid to rest. I did eventually conquer the coefficient of heat in Form 5, just as I finally comprehended Algebra, and in all the years to follow, Algebra proved useful (which I would have studied in Arts anyway), but I have never again solved an equation that applied the coefficient of heat, a number which I cannot for the life of me remember now.

But what I cannot expunge from memory are two moments.

The first was the moment Mrs. Liao was told. She was normally a dignified lady, very attractive and elegant in her *cheongsam*, not tall, with a sweet soprano voice. I can still hear it now as she recited Keats to us, or walked us through our Shakespeare, Dickens and Salinger. Such passion! She loved, no, *adored* literature and she made me adore it too as she took apart the words into metaphor, alliteration, simile, false and real rhymes, the form of the sonnet. As a teacher, she was fair and did not play favorites, encouraging a certain independence of spirit. In Form 3, I desperately wanted her to notice me, but in time came to realize that her notice was not what was important, but rather, that a passionately intellectual embrace of the subject was what mattered. I got my A's because I deserved them, and not because she liked me.

Her face, her habitually calm, controlled face, distorted with rage. Anger creased her forehead; bitterness twisted her lips. Then, the rage subsided. With a deep sigh of resignation, she let me go, and I cannot be sure now, but think I recall her muttering something about *Hong Kong parents think Science is everything,* and if she had, she was certainly not wrong because my mother was merely an extreme example of many Hong Kong parents. What pained me most was that she would not look at me, and after that, I rarely spoke to her again, ashamed that I, one of her star pupils, should have so disappointed her.

Her rage, though, that became my rhythm for the years. You can be grateful to rage that says *you're right, you know you're right, this is not how things should be even if you cannot do anything for the moment* because one day, when life is finally yours to shape, you will draw on her rage and make the life for which you were intended, despite the many missteps along the way. Rage, controlled, frozen, as on a Grecian urn.

There was a second moment, a quieter moment, in the still of the night when Mum was already asleep. In the interest of historical accuracy, despite the fact that memory can never be entirely accurate, I believe it was the night after Sister Rose gave the okay to switch. All I know for certain was that it was a last ditch attempt to salvage myself out of the mess into which I'd landed. *Why had I not said no to Mum, defied her, as I later would do regularly, and often, imposing my will on hers?* Was it ego perhaps? That all the most "intelligent" girls took Sciences? Fear? That unless I acquiesced I would never be "good enough" for my mother, since clearly, I was not her pretty girl, which would have been a different kind of trump card, the way it was and wasn't for my sister, the pretty one. Doubt? That perhaps my mother was right, that I could actually become a doctor, my distaste for Biology notwithstanding. Or was it that the one talent which, as Milton tells, is "death to hide" was lodged in me "useless," this talent I had with words? By fourteen I had published stories and essays in the *South China Morning Post,* publications which only one school friend ever read and noticed. By fourteen I had co-written a serialized story about ouija boards with Annie and a third girl, whom Annie and I cannot remember, that was published in our school newspaper, something none of my classmates now recall. At fourteen, I knew I was only moderately good on the piano and that it was not my destiny, but that writing would remain with me forever. I knew all that, and also knew that the study of Literature was important for someone like me, even if I could not articulate what that "me" was, that useless part of me.

My mother does not read. In her world, tennis and medicine ranked supreme, neither of which engaged me except as mere entertainment or a tedious necessity if I was ill. Two years later, I did fall seriously ill with hepatitis, the infectious kind, and was quarantined in hospital just before I was due to take my medical exam to get a U.S. foreign student visa. My mother was furious then as well, but in retrospect I know her fury was about the weight of too many responsibilities, the lack of money in our family, a disengaged husband and father who had slid into depression. It was not the furious, blind ignorance that forced me into Sciences, into a stream of consciousness mired in quicksand and crocodiles, born of the terror of failure that loomed. My refusal to eat oranges when I was ill also infuriated my mother because she thought I did not want to get well, but my sister sat by my hospital bedside and neatly peeled me oranges once she realized I could not peel without making a mess, the only reason I did not eat the curative fruit.

My mother I have long ago forgiven. You can forgive ignorance, even though it is difficult to do, because knowledge of life is not a prerequisite to being a responsible parent.

The moment, though, that was with Dad. Mum was asleep, because tennis, and victory won by determination, will exhaust the body for slumber, whereas reading the news as my father did or writing stories as I did, only serve to agitate the mind into insomnia. My father was probably smoking a Benson & Hedges out of that golden box with its promise of priceless pleasure. We were, as always, on the verandah, where we gazed at the Hong Kong harbor under a darkened sky, or squinted at constellations through binoculars, and spoke about things my mother did not understand, like why right and wrong were relative unless you believed in an absolute, Catholic God and all His commandments, which I suspected my father didn't, and that I too was beginning to doubt.

He knew, of course he knew, all which had come to pass.

Our conversation circled the subject before landing squarely on its core. "Do you think I should do this?" I finally asked.

He did not answer right away, nor would he look at me. I waited, agitated, frightened but hopeful. The subtext was clear to both of us. *Is she right, am I wrong, is this what life is all about? Tell me, tell me, you're my father. You should know more than me.*

My father glanced up at the sky. "Yes," he said after a few minutes. "You should listen to Mum and take Sciences."

I was fourteen. Eternity was relative. He would not get off that easily and my genes of determination did come from Mum. "Is that also what *you* think?" I demanded, the "you" unmistakably italicized in my tone.

This time, the pause was significantly longer. I could hear the excuses, the circular logic of his debating style, his roundabout prevarications when he didn't want to commit to a viewpoint, the refuge of parental solidarity when we the children were beyond the limit. In the silence of eternal moments, I heard all that he could have said to which he knew I would "cross mouths" with him. Instead, at the end of silence, he looked me in the eye, and said, "Yes, this is what I believe."

Not "we," but "I."

I stared at my father. He had told me the one lie that was unforgivable. In the moment though, you do not analyze, or reflect, or argue. In the moment you only feel the force of betrayal, its fatal wound, and surrender completely because there is no other choice.

The next day, to the astonishment of all my classmates, I walked into 4B, pretending this was all right, taking solace in the celebrity, and settled into the next two years of living, but only just.

And here I am, menopausal and middle aged, when hormones and innocence no longer rule. And I am a writer. Literature invades my waking consciousness; my life is surrounded by the Arts. In the end, two years of adolescent misery do not seem consequential, except as a way of unlocking betrayal.

Over the years I have challenged my mother who acknowledged, reluctantly, that perhaps she was wrong, but only to shut me up rather than through any real revision of belief. There is no reason why she should ever agree with me. She wanted to be a doctor, but couldn't. She believed in the Sciences and their importance to the world. She was not wrong about the fact of science, only in its application to her two older daughters' education. By the time my youngest sister streamed into Arts, as did my brother who was not the academic sort, my mother relented to the force of reality and the limits of her children's talents. Both my younger siblings made good lives, my sister as a criminologist and my brother as a composer, even without the coefficient of heat.

I never challenged my father.

It is only now, after his death, that the ghost of his betrayal visits. It was unforgivable, that act, but he is not unforgiven, because neither he nor I is hostage to an absolute right or wrong, the way my mother tends to be. I do not believe in the forgiveness of sins, because we mortals are not gods, and only gods or the devoutly religious presume to forgive. Blame it on personality, or character that presages fate. It is what we do in Literature after all, which is where I've chosen to live.

forget not

Nay, if you read this line, remember not
The hand that writ it; for I love you so . . .

*from **Sonnet nr. 71 "No Longer Mourn for Me When I Am Dead"***
William Shakespeare

Forget "Not-This"

Note: *Hong Kong (now officially the S.A.R. or special administrative region of the People's Republic of China) comprises an archipelago of 235 islands around a small slice of Southern China. Most of the population lives on Hong Kong island as well as on Kowloon peninsula and the New Territories which make up that slice of the Chinese mainland. Hong Kong covers an area of over 400 square miles. The rural village districts referred to in this essay are in the New Territories.*

On board minibuses, people fall in love, as they do in *Lost in Time*, a 2003 film directed by Derek Yee. Its Chinese title — literally, forget "not-this," the latter idea has no English equivalent — could also be translated as "unforgettable." Surprising, aren't they, the things we cannot forget? If you're like me, you might once have developed a mad crush on someone with whom you shared a minibus ride for a time, a man who remained a platonic friend and fellow rider . . . of course, I was barely twenty-two then, in the midst of an unhappy marriage and therefore prone to mad crushes in alternate realities.

Perhaps, then, it is *appropo* that as a Girl Guide, I belonged to the forget-me-nots patrol. My sister was an orchid, a more appropriate flower since orchids are native to our part of the world, while forget-me-nots are an imagined reality of story books from foreign lands. But there it was, that pale blue *fleur*, with its tiny petals and retiring aspect, gracing my embroidered badge. Character is fate, if we accept the Greek heroic tradition of tragedy as universal, but it seems fate determined the forget-not character that marks me, because to write of Hong Kong, my city of slow dissolve in the early twenty-first century, is a labor of forget "not-this."

And so I remember.

What is it my city insists I not forget? My fellow minibus rider, whose name I no longer dare recall, was a *leang jai,* a Cantonese "beautiful boy" with a flirtatious smile. Our friendship began innocently enough. In Hong Kong of the mid seventies, only a local villager like him or an urban, bohemian madwoman like myself, would live beyond the village of Sai Kung and commute across the harbor to Causeway Bay, at the eastern end of Hong Kong island, each day for work. The journey took approximately two hours and fifteen minutes, one way, weather and unpredictable transportation schedules permitting. I would rise each morning at four or five and try to write, usually unsuccessfully during the months presaging the end of my first marriage. By six it was time to boil water for morning tea and a wash, although the tedium of doing so meant I often willingly elected to take a cold shower. When we first moved into our village home at Tai

Mong Tsai, before a bathroom was installed, I bathed in a nearby stream, clad in my yellow, halter-style swimsuit.

By six-thirty or so, it was out the door, down the path, across the road to where the sea beckoned, to wait on the curb for the bus. The bus was a single-decker, one of the last during Kowloon Motor Bus' metamorphosis into an all double-decker fleet, along this desolate, rural line. It ran once every half hour, more or less. There was no bus stop opposite my home, but drivers on rural routes do stop, the way minibuses also screeched to a halt for a potential passenger frantically flagging it down, with no regard for surrounding traffic. Which was why minibuses met with a legal end, and eventually embraced numbered routes, proper stops, published fares and licenses, because too many fender benders, too much fare gouging, and the rise of a civilized society no longer tolerated this maverick transport, despite the unforgettable love affairs they once ferried.

Back, though, to that original minibus. My day began with a thirty-minute bus ride, plus the wait of ten minutes if I was lucky and Godot's eternity if I was not. There were mornings the bus never appeared, or, being already overloaded, passed me by. On those mornings, I hitchhiked to Sai Kung's central terminus, or even into town if I was exceptionally lucky. The odd private car could occasionally be hospitable. When I was truly desperate, I would awaken my Scottish dog-trainer husband and beg a ride on his motorbike to Sai Kung. All roads led to that village which was where you could board the minibuses headed to Choi Hung's urban central terminus. The same minibus on board which I might, if I were truly blessed, encounter my almost-but-not-quite paramour.

What would life have been like without our crazy, pale yellow minibuses of yore? A semi-legal mode of transport then — meaning it was illegal but tolerated as many things were in our former British colony — these 14-seater vans provided a vital link for the overflow from the legal but hopelessly unreliable public transport system. Just prior to my Tai Mong Tsai life, I lived in Kak Tin Village near Shatin, which still offered a vista of rice paddies and vegetable farms. In our first home there, I washed my hair under an outdoor tap and could not get a telephone line because we were too "remote." Thirty years later, Kak Tin is a suburban enclave of high-rise developments, with flats priced out of the reach of the villagers.

On the main road up the hill from the village, the cross harbor bus number 170 made its last stop before entering Lion Rock Tunnel to Kowloon, which meant I often waited as bus after bus went by, too full to take me, the last rural passenger. There was no minibus. My preferred alternative was to walk half an hour across rice fields along narrow, concrete paths to the Shatin train station. If I was feeling unduly extravagant, $1.40, then the approximate equivalent of one

American quarter, bought me a seat in the first class carriage (or 70 cents in third class, there was no second) of the Kowloon Canton railway to Tsimshatsui by the harbor, where the clock tower was not the lonely structure it is today, surrounded as it was then by an unforgettably romantic red-brick train station. Reminiscent of British war movies, this post-WWII building had been a gift from a colonial taipan, head of one of the "hongs" or major trading enterprises, to grace the city which made him his fortune. At the Star Ferry, I would buy my *South China Morning Post* (or sometimes, the *Hong Kong Standard),* pay my 20 cents to board the first class upper deck as Suzie Wong, that fictional prostitute, once did, sail across the harbor — for longer than the blink of an eye the ride takes today because our waterway is rapidly vanishing — and disembark in Central, the business district, where another minibus would take me to Causeway Bay.

The minibus. This was the fastest, most efficient and reliable transport because it was a profit-making, small business enterprise. Drivers needed to earn their daily rice bowl, unlike the salaried drivers of legal public transport. If one minibus was full, a second appeared quickly so that passengers wouldn't have to wait. There was something cryptically magical about its route network. To get from A to B, you asked someone who knew or hailed a passing vehicle that displayed a hand-scrawled sign with the Chinese characters for B, or somewhere that was on the way to B. There were no maps, no published schedules, no stops, no central telephone inquiry line, no pre-determined tariff, no website. English residents, most of who did not speak or read the language of 98% of the population, complained the loudest about this "dangerous" mode of transport. But the minibus was all about a human network passing the word along, and drivers charged what the market would bear. The minibus was the cheaper alternative to taxis.

The minibus, when it first appeared in the sixties, was the daring, renegade burst of speed in a city growing like Alice on mushrooms, limbs askew, shooting out of control, with insufficient space for movement. The minibus was what "responsible" grown ups like my parents told teenagers *not* to ride, but at fourteen and fifteen, my sister and I found them thrilling. Ever fearful we might have boarded the wrong one, we prayed a policeman would not be at the corner where we wanted to disembark because if so, the driver had to keep going so as not to risk a fine or arrest.

My Sai Kung minibus was the one comfortable leg of a prolonged commute. There always was a seat, unlike aboard the bus from Choi Hung to Star Ferry that followed, where "standing room only" was commonplace. My minibus did not stop at point after point, the way a bus must, prolonging an already tedious ride. The minibus started its journey with a full load, dropped off the odd passenger along the way who was invariably replaced by a new one. Most of us

traveled from terminus to terminus, generally ensuring a non-stop, forty-five-
to fifty-minute ride. When Continental launched the first New York to Hong
Kong direct flight, I quickly pledged allegiance, abandoning my loyalty to
Northwest's Tokyo stopover flight. Old habits die hard, but memories allow us
a sweeter refrain, gracing our passage towards that other eternity. The drivers
on that Sai Kung route came to know you, the regular passengers, and said *jo
sun* to greet the morning, making each day slightly easier to bear.

How did he and I begin our conversations? I no longer know. All I do know
is that he appeared with a few other guys on several mornings, and eventually,
he was the one who always sat beside me. We joked a lot about everything and
nothing, and pretended we did not look into each other's eyes when we did. Our
friendship extended to wild rides in overloaded, souped up cars along Sai Kung's
winding, narrow, coastal road, because these guys lived on the edge, Kerouac-
like, wild and untamed, the way my heart felt then. He was the one with whom
I had my Hong Kong Cinematic Love Affair, full of longing looks, unspoken
words and arrested desires to fuel the long, sad, summer nights. He knew my
husband. That was enough for us to keep our hands to ourselves.

I had my affair instead with an errant *gwailo* Englishman who also knew
my husband, and eventually walked out on my marriage. I moved back into
the city, thus ending those minibus rides. After that, I did not see my *leang
jai* again.

Forget-me-nots grow in my New Zealand garden now, hidden under the front
porch, pale blue and delicate, as promised in the story books.

So what is it *really* that I am commanded not to forget?

That it is not easy to fall in love, on minibuses or anywhere, except perhaps
on screen. Isn't it the same with the vanished past we profess to love, that we
record in order not to forget? Why is it that the gigantic elephant and a tiny
flower are our tropes of remembrance? *Remember, remember, the fifth of
November,* we intoned as children, liking the rhythm of the words without
attention to their meaning. It was almost Guy Fawkes Day when I called it quits
on my troubled, mismatched eighteen-month first marriage. Hong Kong was
not the place to be local, cross-cultural and extra marital back in the seventies,
as our silver screen knows only too well. But we remain, as in Wong Kar Wai's
visual feast, "in the mood for love" despite it all, transforming our lost world
into art, insisting, over and over, *forget not-this, forget not-this.* So recall,
recollect, remember. Minibuses, the tedium of public transport, those rural fields
of leafy greens — *choi sum, tong choi, gai laan* — and rice paddies from when
Hong Kong's villages still strived for self sufficiency to feed our hungry masses.
At least we kept the Tsimshatsui clock tower, and the cross-harbor Star Ferry
still runs, but who knows for how much longer before these too are swallowed

up by greater China and the even greater world that forgets, that so easily forgets all this?

It is late spring, and the humidity of rain clouds has already begun to creep into my sinuses. I am listening to RTHK Radio 3. "Uncle" Ray Cordeiro, that deejay of my forever who at seventy-plus still spins jazz and night time nostalgia, signed off over two hours ago. Music through the night brings me to a little past four, back to the enchanted writing hour that my body does not forget. Yesterday, I watched *Anna Magadalena*, a film of unrequited love to which scriptwriter Ivy Ho brings an exceptional poignancy. This 1998 independent film feels very Hong Kong, the way I feel my city. The protagonist transforms his longing for an upstairs neighbor — she has fallen in love with his crazy friend, a man who reads Kerouac — into a fantasy story of the land of H, where he and his fair maid become "X & O," two orphans who go on their quest for treasure that they donate to the poor in their Asian Nottingham. The story becomes his first book, and it makes possible a love that remains impossible in life.

As if to oblige the fates, the radio plays "Stop in the Name of Love," a signal, I suppose, to stop writing of my vanishing city, to let go of the past and its dissolving dance. Nostalgia does not become us, we diehard citizens of yesterlife who must live Hong Kong of today. Minibuses race all over our cityscape now, along routes to new-and-improved city-villages, to places I have yet to see, to lives and loves I have yet to know.

AERIAL REVERIE

Airport restaurants were romantic in my childhood. We would see Dad off to Kai Tak, and in the wait time (before executive lounges were *the* place to go), the family would have a Cantonese dinner. The taste of crispy fried noodles, covered with pork and vegetables in a steaming sauce, straight from the *wok,* still tantalizes my tongue. The airport was the rare place we would eat Cantonese, as opposed to the northern cuisine my father preferred.

At the Cincinnati airport (which is actually in Kentucky, not Ohio), on a November afternoon in 2005, there are two restaurant choices that are not fast food: Wolfgang Puck's and the steakhouse. At Newark, a New York City airport which is actually in New Jersey, since renamed Liberty International in the wake of 9-11 patriotism, there is a steakhouse at the Continental Airline terminal. Everything else is inelegant, fast food, cheap. It is not that the steakhouses and

Wolfgang Puck's are elegant, but the food will at least resemble something prepared by human hands, as opposed to manufactured on an assembly line and reheated in a microwave.

And so this reverie for an era of air travel when children could wave their father off from an open-air observation deck as he walked across the tarmac to a plane in a major international city, although Hong Kong wasn't quite a "major" city then. Cathay Pacific was a medium-sized regional airline and not the behemoth of today; Pan American and B.O.A.C. (British Overseas Airways Corporation, a.k.a. "Better on a Camel") were among the major international carriers that stopped by. Kai Tak was a quiet airport, for dignified departures and arrivals. Flying was an extraordinarily civilized way to travel, just as working for an airline, in any capacity, was a privileged job for non-beleaguered professionals. Could we have imagined that a few decades of human time would transform all that, in step of course with Hong Kong's metamorphosis from a small colonial city to a large international city-village?

My first arrival into Chep Lap Kok was a strange moment of sadness and pride. The patriot (or was it the jingoist?) said, *finally, an airport that reflects the great city we've become, one we can show off to the world.* Despite operational teething problems, the new airport did live up to its promise, rivaling Singapore's super efficient hub, matching what Heathrow or Schipol or Atlanta or Detroit could offer to the airline industry and its passengers. It took Narita's expansion a few years to catch up. Beijing, of course, has the Olympics to fund the upgrade.

Why sadness for the loss of a perilously located airport? Kai Tak was famous to pilots the world over for its reclaimed runway, a perfect rectangle jutting out to sea. The airway leading towards it required a tricky navigation through building-covered hillsides and the densely populated Kowloon City district, forcing landings and takeoffs that required precision and tight turns, offering the spectacle of almost-crashes into a teeming, human anthill. Yet despite its potential for danger, Kai Tak's safety record was stellar. In the years of its existence as Hong Kong's airport, there were only a handful of fatal accidents. China Airlines once managed to skid off the runway, immersing part of the craft in the sea; it was to make a much worse landing during a typhoon later at Chep Lap Kok. Taiwan's national carrier, which China Airlines is, enjoys as hapless a fate as its foreign relations in this era of "one China."

Perhaps it is the *potential*. There is more than mere nostalgia or romance in the idea of human potential, which is what Kai Tak conjures. Messrs. Kai and Tak were risk takers, just as Messrs. Farrell and Kantzow, the American and Australian founders respectively of Cathay Pacific — the call letters CX slipping into "almost sex" — dared to imagine flying "over the hump" of Burma, turning a maverick cargo airline into an air travel dream. By the time we were ready for an airport like Chep Lap Kok, life was mired in economic assessment, feasibility studies, vision by committee.

Perhaps such potential allows mavericks to be visionary, fostering energy and daring in people, hence creating a city. Isn't that where pride really matters? Not in the self-satisfied, smug, somewhat jingoistic bragging rights we exercise over our new international world-class airport, but in a self-pride that envisions our future and does the job well towards making it happen, by accepting the risk? Isn't that what we need to ensure our city continues to be something we build because it is *ours,* and not because we expect some greater power to take care of everything for us? Wasn't that why we no longer used the term "colony" by the eighties, even though we were to remain under British rule for almost two more decades, because even the pretence of self-determination was preferable to none at all?

I used to be an airline employee. Actually, I worked for two carriers: Federal Express which is all about cargo, and Cathay Pacific Airways, which virtually defines "airline" now. In 1976, the year I joined Cathay, there were three ways into the coveted position as a Chinese employee with potential for management, via job titles such as "officer" or "superintendent," the two ranks below an assistant manager. The stellar path was that of a management trainee, open principally to graduates of Chinese University and the University of Hong Kong; English counterparts (the "Swire princes") came from Cambridge and Oxford. The second way was up through the ranks, especially in the operational areas. These folks in customer service, sales, ground and inflight operations *et al* are really the lifeblood of any airline. The third way, which was my means of entry, was via the back door, a.k.a. timing, timing and luck. Despite a degree from an American university, I was not as lucky as those with the right pedigree who landed among the management trainees (there were a handful of Swire princes from Durham or other such "lesser" institutions at the time as well). However, I happened to meet an English personnel manager who knew of a potential opening in marketing administration where the manager might, he thought, be amenable to someone with advertising experience and good English, my two assets. The trick was "potential": an existing staff member had to be terminated for the job to be available.

Even though I was young, impetuous and poised for risk, I suspected the back door was probably not the best way to advance a career. It was however what fate presented, and who are we to argue with a higher authority? The first week in my new job as a "marketing administration officer," my English boss informed me that I was to go for orientation training, a week-long course with a written test at the end required of all new hires. He also informed me that I would score at least 95% on the test, since even his secretary had done that.

So there I was, back in "school," being taught how to decipher airline tickets, accept reservations, check in customers, read airport codes, calculate travel time between time zones, adapt my sense of time to the 24-hour clock, understand the CX route map, destinations and fleet, memorize the industry's alphabet ("Bravo Whiskey" was code for "bomb warning" in airspeak) and take a multiple choice test at the end. The average employee of any major carrier today does not necessarily even know where the airline flies. Jobs are finely calibrated and specialized so that a reservations staff wouldn't have the faintest idea how to check in a customer. Of course, this was pre-desktop computing, which meant that seats on board were assigned in much the way your theatre ticket was, by a check mark or sticker on a printed seating plan. Human beings made decisions to avoid seating three passengers in a row if there were empty seats elsewhere, rather than allowing a computer to think for them. Were flights on time and late? Were passengers satisfied and unsatisfied? Could an airline function pretty much as airlines today function? Yes, yes and yes. The only difference was the human dimension, because an employee at virtually every level could be expected to be more personally responsible, since greater autonomy was granted the individual to make decisions. Likewise, an employee could be expected to know a great deal more about the business and customer service, because generalists, not specialists, was the nature of work, and information was not as overwhelmingly data, as it is today.

So a song, then, for the individual human spirit which had more room to flourish and breathe in big-city-village Hong Kong, because we were already getting "bigger" then, though nowhere as big as now. I remember the shock on first encountering the American air travel industry. I was sent to a customer relations conference, since part of my job was to respond to customer complaints. The company used to investigate each complaint, the results of which would be reported to the customer in a letter, signed by a manager. Similarly, all letters of praise for our service received a written response thanking the "pax" or passenger. The writing of such letters was a rotating job which went to the newest flunky in the ranks, and somehow, this ended on my desk. My task was to initiate and follow up all investigations, draft the letters, get these typed by the typists' pool, proofread and send the final, correct version to my manager for signature. Modern-day customer relations would scoff at this waste of time since "auto-reply" emails suffice for most communiqués, replete with misspellings, bad grammar and inattention to the actual customer complaint (Mrs. Wong complains: "You sent my luggage to New Delhi even though I was flying to Beijing." Company replies: Dear Mr. Chan, Thank you for your comment which we were very pleased you flew with us. Have a nice day!). Should we mourn the passing of such "time-wasting" jobs in our service industries?

But back to the shock, which was the point of this reminiscence about a vanished world.

I was feeling extraordinarily privileged. There I was, on my first real "business trip" to a conference in Manila, listening to my counterparts in the *really big* airlines talk about "customer relations." The hotel was unimaginable luxury, the free food and booze like manna for a young and struggling yuppie, and economy travel was almost as comfortable as business in airlines today. As switched on as I pretended to be, at the end of the three-day affair, I realized it had all been gobbledygook. The chatter was about computerizing solutions and performance measurements and nothing about the human face of managing customer relations I had expected to learn. Perhaps I sensed that the future would be the shock of the impersonal. If so, it seemed a bleak vision. Later, when I flew to the U.S. and discovered customer service numbers that rang and rang and rang unanswered (the record was thirty minutes), but which were numbers you had to call to reconfirm your flights (a quaint notion these days except on airlines of far flung micro island nations, surrounded by crystalline blue lagoons, serviced by one flight a week), I wondered if the medium-sized carrier I worked for would one day face those same challenges of market growth, the limits of technology and a beleaguered work force.

Shock often arises from innocence, and I was naïve in my CX days. If, however to be naïve is to dream of fulfilling human potential, then perhaps a little nostalgia and reverie has its place in our fast-changing, world-class city, along with its global home airline and fancy new airport.

The first time I sat in a cockpit for landing into Kai Tak, I had sent my business card to the pilot to request this privilege sometimes accorded to airline staff. It was a quietly thrilling experience. Strapped in, a little to the left behind the pilot, I had a clear view of the sky ahead. The flight engineer was more or less beside me, the first officer diagonally opposite, checking his readings. The space felt strangely large for the narrow 707. Later, the cockpits of the larger 747's or Lockheed 1011's struck me as cramped. We circled round, we swooped past hillside housing, and then I saw the runway. My heart beat faster — fear, disbelief, the sensation of the split second that could go wrong — before we landed perfectly. I could have sat there forever.

But it was takeoffs I learned to love, because taking off held the potential for the unknown. I sat in the cockpit less often for takeoffs, but often enough to recall the surge, like a wave carrying you forward, and I think, perhaps this is what it feels like to surf or snowboard or parachute out off a plane, all those physical experiences beyond my ken.

Then 9-11 ravaged airlines and airports worldwide. A person would be crazy to think she could sit in a cockpit now to experience, vicariously, the fiction of flying. The romance of travel has blunted. The way we are may not be the way we used to be, but the way we could be hovers, its potential beckoning, summoning visionaries.

My romance of long-lost family dinners is of small concern. Let us hope that there will always be another maverick with yet another vision of the "perfect" way to fly. Reveries drift through our psyches as long as we choose to ponder, ruminate, dream a little. It could be worse. We could still be galley slaves, rowing with Zhang-he, Magellan or Columbus to the old-new world, without movies or seat belts, and only the amazing speed of wonder.

CONVERSATION SPACE

I have a Cantonese friend with whom I converse. This should be an oxymoron in this city, because how else do we converse with friends except in Cantonese or "Canto-Ching-lish"? But this friend is unique because we converse in a Cantonese that is both our "native-but-not-exactly-first" language, and our friendship comprises these conversations that occur because I visit his bookshop, one that specializes in Chinese art. When Cantonese fails us, he reaches for a Putonghua (Mandarin) equivalent and I for English, at which point we consult one of the many dictionaries on his shelves. His spoken English is halting, limited to words or phrases, and my spoken Putonghua is clumsy, often lost in translation; we both read better than we speak each other's "native" language. Of course, since the handover, our city is supposed to be tri-lingual, claiming Cantonese, Putonghua and English as our tongues, or so the government claims.

Linguistics names our brand of conversation "code switching." Only academics could come up with this idea of "code," as if the language of friends is some mysterious, hidden means of conveying messages among a secret society. It makes me feel a little like a spy. In some ways, I suppose I am, because my friend and I, through these code-switching conversations, are privileged to "spy" upon each other's lives, so separate but equal, so removed from the other save for the intimacy of our conversation space.

I met Kar-Ning because I finally entered his shop, sometime in late '95. Early the next year, I downsized to a flat downhill on Aberdeen Street, in a bid to lower my rent; I wanted to save enough money to quit my job at *The Asian Wall Street Journal* and lead a "real writer's life," meaning without a full-time corporate position but financially liquid enough to feast in a garret. Prior to that, I occupied a "luxury" flat on Robinson Road which was damp with mold and where mosquitoes nightly drank my blood. The point is, all these spaces were along a hillside, more or less parallel to each other, and it was my habit to walk the mile or so from my office and then uphill each evening after work, which was cheaper and less tedious than the stair master at a gym.

The wooden white sign on the pavement with its red lettering in English and Chinese for "Tai Wan Art Books" (in Chinese, literally: "Big Freight Art Bookstore") regularly caught my eye. It was on Aberdeen, several doors below my flat. I had noticed it when I lived on Robinson and had meant to stop in. But my life was consumed — as lives in my city often are — in my case by work, divorce, the writing of fiction, frequent business trips, and a muddled affair with an on-again-off-again Chinese lover whose Putonghua often gave me headaches whenever he chose to visit from up north. His wife and children gave me ulcers, the idea of them I mean, but that's a different story. In this way, months passed, and I would remind myself to stop in and see what the shop was about.

There was nothing particularly extraordinary about the day I finally entered. It was a Saturday afternoon, I believe, but memory is unreliable and chronological exactitude an unnecessary hobgoblin in the telling of tales. The shop was up a flight of stairs in a single room, approximately 100 feet square, perhaps slightly larger, with a bank of windows overlooking the street. It had once been a *tong lau,* a residential "Chinese flat" in an old-fashioned shop house, which means the building was solid concrete, the stairwell dank but cool in summer or dark to morbid in winter if you were an imaginative child.

Shelves lined the other three walls which were packed with books. These were mostly large, coffee-table size art volumes or odd-sized volumes of the historical or theoretical variety. Under the bank of windows were low shelves filled with smaller books, as well as Chinese ink brushes and other paraphernalia associated with calligraphy and painting. In the center of the room was a rectangular island of shelves with a table top counter awash in a sea of yet more books. At the far end of the island was a desk, at which a well-built, slender, middle aged Cantonese man sat reading, his back to the windows. On subsequent visits, I would almost always come upon him reading, or occasionally, practicing calligraphy. He will look up, rise, break into a grin, exclaim my full name in Cantonese and say, "so you're back again." This is Kar-Ning, who moved his life from Beijing to Hong Kong in the eighties.

On that first visit, he looked up in acknowledgement, welcomed me to his shop, and left me to browse. The majority of books were in Chinese, although there were a few bi-lingual volumes. I found a couple of the latter that would be a useful addition to my own library. These I purchased, and, as a result of this single, commercial transaction, our conversations began.

It would be impossible to record the hours of talk that flew around our space. Initially, we spoke of our lives, exchanging personal histories and family tales. We were both divorcing, a contemporary exercise that brings people together while driving marriages apart. It was rare to be able to speak frankly to a Chinese man about marriage and divorce, and our early conversations dwelled on the simultaneously guilty and innocent consciousness that the ones who provoked the split must balance. He has two daughters, I have no children, but the thing that connected us was the need to speak to someone else who also bore the "stigma" but would not judge the other harshly. Between us, we could leave that stigma unsaid.

Does our enforced use of a "not-exactly-first language" medium create or obscure truth? Our exchanges are blunt but civilized. In the early conversations, we spoke of infidelity, post-marital sexual abstinence and lust, the inability to develop satisfactory relationships in Hong Kong. Over the course of my friendship with Kar-Ning, I ended the unsatisfactory affair with my Beijing lover and eventually cemented a far more satisfactory relationship with my New York man. He, meanwhile, found someone with whom he could enjoy a relationship after a long spell of brief, unsatisfactory encounters. We update each other on our lives when we meet. The unique spatial encounter allows us to recognize the true condition of the other because we are usually correct when we say, *you look healthy* or *you look worn,* followed by, *so what's happening in your life?*

But we speak of other subjects beyond the movement of our lives. I am particularly interested in his take on Hong Kong, which is the closest to my father's attitude I've ever encountered. Dad was, like Kar-Ning, a "Chinese foreigner" in the city, an immigrant who arrived from China as an adult and remained the next forty-nine years until his death, all the while ensuring that he would not stumble down the same path as the unfortunate locals.

Their attitude can best be described as one that embraces *a state of absence* regarding Hong Kong. Neither man believes that this city, meaning its government, culture, ethos or existence, can truly embody meaning for a people, by which, I imagine, each means himself. One of the best examples is language.

As a child, I would sometimes hear Dad speak Mandarin to friends and associates. He was proud of his fluency, and welcomed opportunities to converse with others equally as "civilized." Cantonese was to his ear and tongue barbaric, and my siblings and I delighted in our Canto-lish code switching, enhanced by Pig Latin and French, which neither parent could fully comprehend. Years later, when I pointed out to my father that the roots of ancient Chinese are more evident in modern Cantonese than Mandarin, he would look at me slightly askance as if I were that tiresome adolescent to whom he must pay some, but not total, attention.

Yet Dad and I found our conversation space, usually around four in the morning on our verandah.

For years I've enchanted audiences and the media with the story of my youthful "awakening." At the age of eleven, I awoke one morning at four and crept out to our verandah. The sight of Hong Kong harbor by night was so beautiful, calm and entrancing that I wrote an essay right then and there which became my first published piece. We storytellers are an amoral lot; we know what audiences like to hear and repeatedly conjure a flattering image of ourselves in our desire to be "good copy." For all the truth of that first awakening, which led to a lifetime of early morning writing, the story that is harder to tell is the one of the noise in your head, the voices that shriek and will not leave you alone, the fury and shouting that keep you awake in search of the relief that only writing seems to bring.

In such an insomniac's fit did I first discover my father, sometime within a few months of the first awakening.

Dad often went to bed late, well after my mother, and stayed up into the morning hours reading or, as I eventually came to understand, reflecting on life. We lived on the top two floors of Far East Mansion on Middle Road, where my parents had purchased these two narrow flats and constructed an interior stairwell to connect them. The bedrooms were upstairs and the downstairs living and dining room opened out onto a long, open, "suicide-jumper" verandah which used to face the Hong Kong harbor. The building has survived demolition, but looks worse for the wear, especially now when surrounded by shiny new towers and renovated hotels. It still faces the harbor, what little we have left of it, but no longer has a view, blocked as it was years ago by the Sheraton Hotel. I keep tabs on the top floor lounge of that hotel, visiting it now and then to reclaim the sights of childhood.

The morning I encountered my father on our verandah, I felt like an intruder coming upon another. To my girlish eyes, the tiny downstairs space by night was cavernous (there was possibly 200 sq. ft. of usable space, plus an impossibly cramped kitchen). But it was not a space to be shared when everyone was supposed to be asleep. Once I'd found that "room of one's own," I selfishly deemed it mine, at least for a couple of hours before creeping back to bed.

Dad looked at me in surprise. He had finished his nightly scotch — this was likely the second glass he consumed if he was still up — and asked me what I was doing. I told him the truth, that I sometimes woke up and wrote in the mornings. That first encounter was brief: he nodded, told me not to stay up too late and then went to bed.

What I recall is that I wasn't afraid of my father by night. When my sister and I were very young, aged three and four, Dad could be irascible, impatient, angry at noisy and uncontrollable children. We were hit for being naughty, and felt the sting of his bare hand; in the worst case, Dad whipped us with the bamboo rod of the feather duster until my mother intervened and put a stop to this form of punishment.

But by age eleven, when my father's business had begun its irreversible downslide, I already suspected that he was in fact a gentle man who loved music and learning but could not change the path of his life. He could still be a stern parent by day, insisting on quiet the moment he got home at which point Mum would send us the children upstairs to our room to continue the fracas. Yet he could be lively at dinner if he were in a good mood, engaging us all in conversations ranging across subjects from the minute to the gargantuan. After dinner, he even was known to play Monopoly with the family, which is the main reason I learned the streets of London. So I was not afraid of him by night, in the "half-late third watch" time that is the Chinese equivalent of "graveyard shift" or the "wee hours." He was like a shadow man, who did not dictate the way a parent would, who treated me as if I were another shadow being floating past him in the red dust of the space-time continuum. And I suppose we were shadow beings, even then, since my later life would take me far away from my parents, often for years without a physical meeting. It was the beginning of the insomniac's life, approved of by my father, and the absurdly powerful reality of those early morning encounters would shriek me awake in multiple cities and towns on various continents, out of warm beds, away from the warm body beside me, in order to write and embrace my *raison d'etre*.

It is the pleasurable sensation of conversation I always recollect, rather than the actual words spoken. With Dad, and later friends like Kar-Ning, I knew the importance of words shared about the puzzle of life, regardless of our physical experiences. Through the ravages of puberty, when I learned that I was not the pretty Chinese girl I once imagined myself as a child, but instead an odd, too-dark-complexioned being that Hong Kong Chinese boys didn't quite know what to do with, Dad would appear in our phantom encounters and I could speak of something other than the painful life of the flesh. Did God exist (my mother was staunchly Catholic, my father barely so)? Was love a real or imagined delusion? Why was philosophy the subject I absolutely must take at university (this was the one firm idea regarding education my father expressed)? Did corporal life matter in the slightest and if so, why? And why the hell did we have to live in Hong Kong anyway?

Because Hong Kong, with its stunningly gorgeous harbor view by night, seemed only a preparation for something else back then. My father spoke lovingly of Shanghai, where he had spent one term at St. John's University before fleeing in 1949, an unfortunate year for Chinese capitalistic jazz-playing students from Indonesia. He described a traditionally classic schooling in Indonesia that prepared him for tertiary education in China. He invoked other harbors — San Francisco, Rio de Janeiro, Copenhagen — from his actual and armchair travels. He made it clear that my future did not belong in Hong Kong, an idea I both savored and resisted.

As a teenager, I could not articulate the resistance, only the longing to be someplace else. Yet all memories of our conversation space bring me home to Hong Kong, time and again, and to that harbor. Even Kar-Ning draws me back with his new-and-improved "Big Freight" space to converse over tea and oranges. He overlooks Lyndhurst Terrace now instead of the police residential quarters on Aberdeen, having moved around the corner from law enforcement to the historical red light district. Today, Lyndhurst is a busy commercial street of camera shops, art galleries, framers, chic restaurants, my one-time favorite stationers, along a sloping street near the harbor, a street which once was virtually the waterfront before reclamation.

Do we uncover meaning in conversations about the roots of our hearts? To converse requires that other person, in ghostly or other demarcations. Near the end of his life, my father spoke of Hong Kong as a city that had everything he needed. He visited me once in New York during the late eighties and was disappointed by the lack of modernity, the crime and filth, the inefficiency and sheer unmanageability of it all. By then, Hong Kong seemed so much more modern, desirable, livable. By then, Hong Kong was his home.

Like Kar-Ning, my father perpetually disdained local concerns, and continued to do so even as he acknowledged the city as his space in time. Dad had a lifelong interest in politics generally, and regularly read several local papers — he took all the English morning and afternoon dailies back in the sixties (the *South China Morning Post, Hong Kong Standard, China Mail* and *The Star);* in Chinese he initially subscribed to the *Wah Kiu Yat Pao,* but in later years switched to the pro-Communist *Wen Wei Pao* plus the *Sun Maan Pao* (New Evening News) until the latter ceased publication. He watched ATV World and TVB Pearl English television news, which are broadcast simultaneously, taping one while viewing the other, but never was comfortable with Cantonese electronic media. As well, he read the *Far Eastern Economic Review,* glanced at both *Time* and *Newsweek,* and maintained a subscription to *Kompas,* the Indonesian daily. Yet in his later years, I could never interest him in anything fostered by either Governor Patten or Tung Chee-hwa (he dismissed both men as ignoble and ignorable), and to him, Hong Kong's political existence was simply an aberration. There are no "real Chinese" here, he believed, something Kar-Ning appears, at times, to echo. But both men are themselves a funny-peculiar breed of Chinese — Dad a mixed-race Fujianese-Javanese who speaks a different dialect from the vast majority of the local populace; Kar-Ning a Cantonese who speaks his "own" dialect with a slight Putonghua accent, although he has by now learned our slang and Cantonese script so that local newspapers are comprehensible.

Had my father ever met Kar-Ning, he would initially have liked conversing in the rolling tones of Beijing Putonghua. They both would probably have delighted in abhorring Hong Kong, eventually tempering their remarks by what they do appreciate of the city, since they are both reasonable men. They would likely share a vaguely pessimistic outlook as to the future of "Xianggang." Yet what would puzzle Dad would be the very existence of this man, Kar-Ning, another "Chinese foreigner in Hong Kong," a man a little like himself, who also pays tribute to the Chinese tradition that shaped him, one that allows him to survive in the foreign mud that has become "home." Perhaps they will meet someday in the red dust, high above the skies of Hong Kong, and converse as civilized people will, without the strictures of time and space.

I wished for many more verandah conversations with my father, but grown up daughters leave home, our family sold that space years ago, and now, the view has changed dramatically. I wanted to tell Dad that cities have cycles, that even New York recovered and became newer, cleaner, more livable, but he died before I could.

He visits me still, always when I'm back in Hong Kong, startling me awake from dream-sleep in the early morning hours. His visits are benignly normal, without the painted-white, gory, *gwai* images of Chinese cinema billboards that haunted my childhood. He usually says something about life when he visits; the very familiarity of those encounters takes me back to our verandah and harbor. In the mornings, I know he will always be there, and that our conversation space is eternal.

space break

It's made of sticks
Sticks and bricks
But you can get your kicks
In the house of bamboo

from **House of Bamboo (1958)**
Music and Lyrics by Bill Crompton *and* Norman Murrells
Recorded by Earl Grant (1960)

A Glossary of Evanescent English from Our Shores

"Gloss it," says my academic linguistics friend. He uses "gloss" the way I use "plot" in the construction of fiction, transforming the noun into a verb, narrowing its meaning to a writer's craft technique, directing a student who needs advice for a story or novel.

Gloss. Such a beautiful, transitive verb. Its sound evokes the transparent glare of glass as well as the glorious romance of glow. To gloss is to give something a deceptively attractive appearance. But if we choose to transition the noun into a verb, to gloss then becomes to illuminate the hidden meaning behind a complex or difficult idea, thus enriching and enlarging its possibilities in the imagination. Hong Kong English is one such complex idea, a notion that neither academics nor ordinary citizens can entirely embrace. English was once the *only* official language of Hong Kong, and it remained so until the seventies when Cantonese was accorded the same status. A rather late date for the language of the masses.

Neverrrrmind, as Rosannadanna used to say, the fictional TV character on *Saturday Night Live* played by the late Gilda Radner, a talent evanescent too young, too soon. What's done is done, what's past is went and will not be going anywhere unless, at the very least, we preserve the past for future, puzzled generations, should they choose to gaze back at pieces of the whole, in an attempt to reconstruct a fuller picture.

Record it, recall it, write it.

Gloss it.

Journey to Beijing is a documentary by filmmaker Evans Chan that chronicles a 1997 walkathon from Hong Kong to Beijing, the purpose of which was to raise funds for literacy in China. The walk becomes the cinematic path for a discussion about the handover, through interviews with some of the walkers and their families, as well as with an eclectic range of artists, filmmakers, politicians, and social, political, environmental or cultural activists.

In the film, one of the walkers says that some of the people he met in China expected Hong Kongers to speak English. They were surprised to meet these Chinese beings who were "like them." If we Hong Kong citizens could be that shockingly unknown only a decade earlier to folks in the "inner territory," the way the Mainland is sometimes referred to in Chinese, how far can we really have gone on our city's voyage towards Beijing?

Yet we cannot deny our rather unusual English language legacy, neither its colonial roots historically, nor its prevalent and continued usage in the global commerce that marks our city. The language sequence of public announcements and telephone information recordings is perhaps the most telling comment on our linguistic culture: first Cantonese, then English, and then Putonghua. Sometimes, the latter two are reversed, but just as often, English "walks first," as we say in Cantonese.

Hence this glossary of English and almost English, one that does not pretend to be anything more than a space break in this journey of memory and moment.

The Glossary of Evanescent English

ABC neither the alphabet nor a media company, just as neither are **BBC** nor **CBC** nor **NBC**, these acronyms used to identify the passport or birth origins (i.e.: American, Australian, British, Canadian, New Zealand), although often incorrectly so, of any ethnic Chinese person who does not look, move, speak, behave sufficiently Chinese enough for local tastes; the list is probably expanding faster than can be tracked.

Asian Values a useful fallback position that has been vetted by supposedly superior minds for those who cannot *bear* anything Western to be of value.

Basic Law an idea that is already past its sell-by date.

Canto-pop perhaps the only truly authentic Hong Kong music.

Censorship a non-existent state in this wild and crazy place where "anything goes" until someone complains and the *wok* must be shouldered.

China daily 24-7, non-stop, incessant, "you are always on our minds."

Chief Executive (Manufactured English) formerly, Running Dog.

Christianity a safe Western precept for Hong Kong politics, unlike Marxism.

Colony the quaint condition of the city's existence for some 150 years that anyone under the age of twenty-one might find exceedingly foreign unless used as a synonym for the S.A.R.

Critic a breed under threat of extinction that should be signaled for wildlife conservation.

Dai wok (Cantonese) lit. "big *wok*" meaning the Chinese hemisphere pan which cooks who know what they're doing use to sauté, steam, boil, poach, deep fry just about anything that walks, crawls, flies, swims; also slang for a major, usually catastrophic, situation, applicable to the city whenever it starts to sink, even temporarily.

Dimsum (Globalish) lit. "touch the heart" Hong Kong's most successful worldwide colonizing strategy, yet to be properly absorbed by the Tourist Board.

Etc.etc.etc.dangdang linguistic root uncertain but a life form which flourishes locally, not unlike *la cucaracha;* secondary etymology in the Chinese verb "to wait."

Expat a web presence on this homepage of a city.

Friend (Canto-Asian-lish) pronounced "frand" or "frrrennnddd" (soft r, sort of rising tone) an uncertain state of being that may or may not equal its English meaning, especially in the wee small hours of *le matin.*

Freedom of speech what local media claims it has.

G.O.D. (Truly Hong Kong English) an acronym, surely, what else could it be?

Gong Wu (Cantonese) or ***Jiang Wu*** (Putonghua) the least evanescent vocabulary there is since marital arts film buffs will archive and preserve those cinematic offerings in which the hell-paradise that is *gong wu* exists.

Gwai (Chinese) lit. "ghost" or "devil" but used in virtual English as a synonym for Westerner.

Hang Seng Index (Globalish) Hong Kong's other worldwide colonizing strategy now that Wall Street is truly 24-7.

HKID (Fictional Language) lit. acronym for "How Kindly I Dream" that you are what you are because you think you are so and now we have a picture and thumb print to prove it.

ICQ (Acronymlish) "I, too, Can handle the Quill," language irrelevant.

Laissez faire (French) lit. "leave" or "allow to do" but so widely understood in Hong Kong as a characteristic of our economy and, some would say, culture, that it might as well be Chinese.

Massacre (American, comparable to Kent State) considered obscene usage by some in this city.

Mickey *Lo Shu* (Chinglish) blurring the distinction between "mouse" and "rat" for that globalized Chinese cartoon character of profit, profit and more profit.

Motherland euphemism for "Benevolence" in common parlance.

MTR (Subversive English) "must travel right" or you might miss the through train.

Onecountrytwosystems synonym for supercalifragilisticexpialidocious, i.e.: "Even though the sound of it is something quite ~~atrocious~~" oops, "~~precocious~~" oops, "precious, of course, *precious,*" the syllabic inconsistency be damned.

Peg (Financialspeak) what neither Chinese currency currently wishes to do without *vis-à-vis* the U.S. dollar.

RTHK (archaic) once a broadcasting entity that was a public *vox pop,* often openly critical of the Hong Kong government; current usage tbd although "Run The Hills Kill" (sung to the tune, badly, of "The Sound of ~~Music~~" oops, "Money") has been advanced by some.

S.A.R. (English, more or less) lit. "Special Administrative Region," the quaint condition of the city's existence since July 1, 1997, sometimes mistaken for a serious respiratory ailment that plagued the city causing a virtual shutdown for a time.

Shanghai Tang (Anglicized Cantonese) lit. the shore of Shanghai, also known as the Bund in English; also, how to be "Oriental" in the West, and not even nostalgically.

Sun Yat-sen local hero of historical significance publicly honored by government funding; also, a resounding failure as a political leader except among his diehard followers.

Tango a uniquely expensive dance form among the jet set in this city costing in the millions in any currency. Go figure.

Tiananmen a large public square in Beijing where the Olympic torch will blaze and which was the site of some historical incidents, we forget what.

Tri-lingualism virtual linguistic reality; a.k.a. wishful thinking.

Uh huh uh huh (Oral Hong Kong English) meaning unclear but often incorrectly mistaken for the affirmative by native English speakers.

Wui Heung Jing (Cantonese) lit. "return to your home village authorization" but local thesaurus allows as synonym for patriotism.

Xenophobia a state of cultural grace to keep unwanted "foreigners," including Mainlanders, out of the city, except as money-spending tourists.

Yan Chinese, literally "person" or "human" but so often used to exclude all but the Han Chinese that anyone who has spent more than a minute in Hong Kong gets the message.

Yuan yang (Spiritual Chinese-English) for kool kats who are into "chinese culture."

1949 in Youthspeak, like, you mean there was *life* back then????????

1967 in olden days, this marks the year of living courageously.

1984 the year of being swept down the river-harbor of iron-lady negotiations.

1997 (Numerology) to be read in any language as a matter of interpretation; also, four numbers that add up to a busted Blackjack hand to prove, beyond an unreasonable doubt, that we were either asleep or illogically incautious after being dealt the first two cards of a winning hand.

2046 a room number of startling insignificance or possibly a year of living indecorously, if not dangerously.

KEY STROKES BY LOONG HEI

Note by author: *These post-'97 op-ed's are by a bi-lingual (Cantonese-English) native of Hong Kong. "International" writers, who do not embrace either the language or ambivalence of the majority, opine and emote on developments in this city till their keyboards are worn, certain their words define a superior moral stance. Loong Hei, whose pen name means "Dragon's Breath," has never been entirely sure that words, or rather "key strokes," should ever carry such weight. Likewise, Loong Hei is uncertain whether pen names, however pseudonymous, do in fact conceal an author's identity.*

July 2002
"Psychological Reversion"

And what would life be like without the morning's dose of *China Daily?* Consider today's report: "Five years after the reunification, the S.A.R. government has done a lot of work to promote cultural identity and *psychological reversion* among its population."

It is mid July and we are hot. The annual celebrations are over, life goes on, but we are now reassured by the establishment of a new Culture & Heritage Commission, the subject of today's news story. Printed words are Serious Business, so I've spent this morning digesting and ruminating over psychological reversion. The headline declares our city's culture is thriving. The writer of the report goes on to quote a local official who says: "Hong Kong culture is part of Chinese culture, a special part," pointing out the "international characteristics" resulting from our colonial past. Hong Kong people are increasingly embracing their Chinese heritage, he says, and the point of such a Commission is to affirm this "self-initiated cultural re-positioning," one which emphasizes "duality." That doesn't sound so bad, does it? We get to be Chinese without letting go of our "pluralistic" side. One culture two cisterns — one big one smaller, China and the rest of the world — into which we will dip and make up a hybrid heritage. How unspeakably "middle kingdom" of us.

Yet how intriguing that this should be labeled "reversion." It brings to mind the idea of a reversal of fortunes, the kind experienced by wealthy feudal landlords in Shanghai before they ran to Hong Kong after 1949. After all, we cannot deny that side of our history, that our little city's fortune, and culture, were built in large measure by such Chinese. Nor can we forget the hordes of freedom swimmers and other escapees of the Cultural Revolution. The descendants of these original Mainland Chinese are the true Hong Kong belongers, born and bred here in this cauldron of Canto-Euro-Chinese-ness, with *laissez-faire* characteristics. Are we ready for such "reversion," psychological, cultural, or otherwise?

It depends, I suppose, on what we mean by "psychology" and "culture," or rather, what *China Daily* means. China's daily urban rice bowl is giving way to the culture of English lessons, Macburgers and private cars, especially among the young. Meanwhile, young Hong Kongers are blurring history ("colony, oh yeah, I think I've heard something about that," a student at an "international college" business course recently quipped in response to his lecturer's remark, "when we were a British colony" to which she received puzzled stares). While China becomes more international, it sometimes seems we are becoming less so. Why else would we need a government commission to ensure our culture and heritage survive? Or were we not really all that international in the first place? Is that duality and hybridity a myth perpetuated by the small, foreign-influenced elite — in government, business and the academic sectors — the tiny percentage who hold a majority of the wealth?

To fully appreciate local culture and psychology, you simply have to ride public transport regularly. On board buses, trams, trains and the MTR, young couples are lost in their *yee yan sai gai,* a two-person world of fatigue. How exhausted all young lovers seem! We'd like to think it's from amorous entanglements but perhaps it's really from clinging so hard to each other out of fear of being torn apart. Younger solo travelers are bent over mobiles, PDA's, comic books, lost inside those worlds. The middle-aged ones keep eyes front, focused on their inner thoughts, avoiding eye contact with all around them. Only the Mainland Chinese look outwards, staring at the ads and other travelers, these over-dressed Chinese in the glitter purchased from our stores. Only they still seem curious, stimulated by the organized chaos of our city, thriving in its many wonders, while the locals fight boredom and exhaustion.

Is this why we need such psychological reversion, to be re-energized by the hunger China has for the world? To play catch up to four thousand years of Chinese cultural heritage because we are already eradicating the last 150 years of our own? Government policy does not a culture or heritage make despite optimistic headlines daily from China ("A Culture to Treasure is Thriving"). We the people must learn to *oi gok* — love the state or nation — in the language of our city, rather than to *ai guo* in the language of the Mainland where the state is always and only China.

On a hot day like today, the cauldron simmers, threatening overflow.

May 2004
Democracy?!? But Sweetie, Wouldn't You Rather Go Shopping?

Perhaps we need a truth, universally acknowledged, that a people long denied democracy must be ill-equipped for its arrival. This seems to be the case today for our citizenry, despite the Basic Law and a colonial history of civil rights and Western-style freedoms. As a native of the city, I cannot help but wonder if something went awry, or if, in fact, it was history that was awry. Perhaps this is the time to reflect, in our present designation as an S.A.R., an acronym to replace the B.C.C. (British Crown Colony). After all, this one-country-two-systems tag for our peculiar political entity supposedly guarantees us autonomy and self governance for fifty years after the "handover" to the Motherland.

What can we say of democracy in Hong Kong?

It has now been seven years since the change, yet every time we scratch that itch, a sore erupts rather than the hoped-for relief.

Under British rule, we the people were *almost* proud to be apolitical. In fact, weren't *we* the pioneer people back then who kept our heads down, worked hard and valued economic growth above and beyond all else? Oh, there was that scuffle in '66/'67 that vaguely resembled a bid for democracy, but the protest, you recall, was against the British. The West aided and abetted happily enough during China's isolationist years, and feasted on Hong Kong's prosperity, without democracy. By the early nineties, North Americans (yes, we also mean you, Canadians) outnumbered British nationals in the "fragrant harbor," these being mostly finance and multinational executives, professionals or academics and their entourages; as well, the "passport migrants" whose return contributed to these numbers. For thirty-something years before the handover, we were *the* party city for global capitalists (yes, we also mean foreign professionals and academics who first helped establish and later lusted after the pig-fat fees and salaries in the government and universities). As the Long March faded in China's collective memory, and to get rich became glorious *à la* Deng Xiaoping, even the elite comrades ventured south to our shores, that Neverland for lost boys, and girls.

Did it feel like democracy then? On the surface of things, we resembled London or New York with our healthily frenetic stock market, transparent accounting standards, rule of law, lack of corruption, post-modern cityscape, civil liberties and civilities. We amused ourselves with our freedom of movement as well-heeled, well-educated, multi-lingual-cultural Hong Kong "nationals," traversed the globe in search of enterprise, education, pleasures. Our press appeared free because, well, we weren't prudish like those up north (*Playboy? Cosmo? Time?* Okay!) and no one got thrown in jail for too long. This was true both during the protests over Tiananmen and the more recent marches for democracy. Who needs the real thing? Disney Democracy was good enough because even when the economy tanked, bird flu invaded, S.A.R.S. terrorized, and little changes insinuated their way into our world (look, ma, it's a sparrow, it's a missile, no, it's the PLA), life was and still is about "fun, fun, fun." And those little changes since the handover aren't all bad. The People's Liberation Army is no less repressive than the British Armed Forces (who lived, by the way, in much finer quarters than their Communist counterparts do); the acculturation towards things Chinese for a populace that is 95% ethnically Chinese is a lot less foreign than singing "God Save The Queen"; and the elite who have ruled and continue to rule us, whether British, Hong Kong Chinese, Communist Chinese or Mickey Mouse all play in the same backyard.

Just what are ex-colonials best equipped for? Neo-colonialism? Unlike those independent Southeast Asian nation states in our backyard, we *didn't* send our British overlords packing (*duh,* was that the problem?). We are some 7 million educated, civilized, financially astute, globally acculturated citizens without a nation, or perhaps even in time, without a political cause. "One country two systems" means we are Chinese nationals of an awkwardly different stripe than those on the Mainland, but unquestionably under China's sovereignty, just as we once were downstairs to England's upstairs (remember, remember those "Hong Kong British passports" that required visas for entry to Britain?). Mother China knows best: favors are granted to those who keep their heads down, work hard, play harder and keep track of the bottom line. Not unlike, as Beijing will be quick to note, the culture in most multinational corporations. After 150-plus years as colonial citizens, surely we've learned a thing or two. Yes, Minister. As you wish, Sir. Politics? Hardly, Minister, not in the S.A.R. Company, Ltd. Incorporation, British and hence Hong Kong style, is all about the limited good. Democracy? Don't bet your rice bowl. There is the racetrack and Macau's casinos are nearby; you don't see them protesting, do you? Now be good boys and girls and go sing *karaoke* or something. Leave politics to those (*oops,* eliminate "~~of us~~") who know better. Yes, dear, puberty is awful but listen, you do get to keep the S.U.V., for now.

October 2005
The Chinese-ness of You

And because it's "National Day," the imperative this Saturday morning which upsets digestion of the *dimsum* with my *jo cha* is this: "Identify Yourself"! It is almost enough to make you cancel your subscription to the *South China Morning Post* in favor of resurrecting the *Eastern Express,* an English daily that was evanescent even before its demise.

Several surveys, it appears, have tried to measure what is described as the "*shifts* in Hong Kong's sense of identity." So surprise, surprise, despite the fact of our "national" day, a day when patriotism should swell our hearts full of Chinese blood, we learn that the majority of survey respondents consider themselves more "Hongkongese" than Chinese. The pundits have much to say about this. Earlier this year, the same local rag reassured us that our city does indeed have its "place" in China, because we are "one nationality, two identities." Everything deflates to politics. If you want universal suffrage, then you are excessively individualistic (read: westernized) and prefer to call yourself "Hongkongese." If however you put the nation first, as any "real" Chinese would, then you will identify yourself as Chinese. Notably, one academic quoted in today's report cites a former Xinhua director who observed of Hong Kong that "while the territory has returned (to China), people's hearts haven't."

How hypocritical, this nationalized concern over identity! There is an archaic definition of the word to mean an "individual or real existence." How refreshing to think that identity could be linked instead to the idea of existence. I exist in this space called Hong Kong from which I consequently derive an identity. Of course, if I happen to be Cantonese or Shanghainese or some other kind of Chinese, or perhaps, not even ethnically Chinese at all, but if I happen to exist here, this space will certainly lay some claim on me. To limit identity to a political or national construct, or to demand that it be a choice certifying loyalty to the nation seems unbearably sad. Identity emerges from who we feel we are, who we have evolved to become over time, and is larger than mere nationality or political bias.

As one former friend often used to say: *Ask me no questions and I'll tell you no lies.*

All this pontificating over survey results, of polls that ask unanswerable questions in the first place, simply masks the absence of critical thought. A more meaningful consideration on this, our national day, would be to reflect on why this day must be celebrated and what bearing that has on us as a people. After all, in the years before the handover, it was not October 1, but October 10, which many Hong Kong people called "national" day. Did that make us traitors because the Nationalist flag flew, because a different way of being Chinese asserted itself among some of the citizenry? Rather than pontificating, shouldn't we examine, honestly, the contradictions of existence, of being human?

For inspiration, let us turn to the Chairman, because he was the man responsible for the Motherland's current form of existence. Among his many thoughts was this treatise: "On the Correct Handling of Contradictions among People" dated February 27, 1957, published approximately a lucky eight years after the founding of the People's Republic in '49. That is roughly the same span of time since we abandoned our British colonial identity to this present moment for a specially administrative Chinese one. As we all know, Mao was a mass of contradictions, and you can only pay attention to his thoughts with measured tablespoons of salt. Nonetheless, this little grain on the handling of contradictions is worthy of attention:

"The only way," he said, "to settle questions of an ideological nature or controversial issues among the people is by the democratic method, *the method of discussion, of criticism, of persuasion and education,* and not by the method of coercion or repression." (*italics, mine*)

Now isn't that interesting? His own actions in later years repudiated that notion, but his words remain to taunt us with possibilities. Of course, Mao is out of fashion these days, especially in "Chinese" Hong Kong, so the local editorial tries instead to convince us that this commemorative day has a "wider significance" for Chinese people to "take pride in being Chinese." In bold type, the polite command is — and as well mannered as the tone may be it is a command rather than a discussion — that this is the day to "celebrate a common bond."

What does it really mean to be an ethnically Chinese person in a special administrative region? Must I wear my Chinese-ness on my sleeve, elevate the connection of blood and ethnicity to the highest level, wave a sunny red flag, sing an anthem in a dialect that is not my mother tongue, exemplify the "healthy development," as one pundit defines it, of a "more balanced attitude towards the Mainland"? We are privileged to be an educated people in a stable, global economy where peace has long prevailed. The fundamental paradox of our state of being has less to do with identity and more to do with what that privilege affords. Call me irresponsible, perhaps, but I believe we would be more responsible in examining the poll result of the 72% who said that "some affairs happening in China make me feel ashamed." If history is any guide, Hongkongese have voted with our feet on many occasions in the past and will again, if strong enough feelings overcome us. Identity is simply not just a national issue.

Grant us, if you will, the right to speak our mind and criticize without fear of imprisonment. Grant us, if you will, the right to say that universal suffrage is something we want and desire for our piece of China. Our Chinese-ness has to do, in part, with the physical proximity of our space. But the emotional proximity, the "identity" that binds us to China, will ultimately arise from being able to see ourselves reflected in the face of the country, in both its mind and heart, and most of all, in a moral conscience of which we are truly proud.

Ai guo, love the nation. We hear this imperative sounded over and over again, as if who we know ourselves to be is not good enough for the nation, that we must deny who we are to become "real" Chinese. This is insufferable nonsense. "Chinese" is an enormous enough concept — historically, culturally, philosophically — to embrace a multitude of voices and ways of being. Anything less would be an insult to the Chinese-ness of us. And no, *we need not always agree.*

If Chinese-ness were a love song, then consider these lyrics from "The Nearness of You," one of the sweetest love ballads ever composed in the opinion of this "Chinese" person:

> When you're in my arms
> And I feel you so close to me
> All my wildest dreams come true.
> I need no soft lights to enchant me if you'll only grant me the right
> To hold you ever so tight, and to feel in the night
> The nearness of you.

>> *Lyrics by* Ned Washington, *Music by* Hoagy Carmichael (1937)

Or if such Western influence is too much foreign mud, then, lest we forget, there is always Mao and his little red thoughts.

March 2007
On a Dreamless Isle

I watch the fadeout of my city-village as I knew it — long before the sheen of meta-globalism and wealth became its second skin — with a mix of nostalgic longing, despair and a tenuous hope. China's gentle giant hand on democracy in Hong Kong ensures that we will eventually be swallowed up and digested by our sovereign ruler, the way the Motherland always intended, despite whatever protest we and the world might register.

The Basic Law that Britain promulgated with China prior to the 1997 "handover" is a blip in yet another of the "unequal treaties" that litter China's history with the West. This time, though, the unequal tips in favor of the People's Republic. Perhaps this is redress, revenge of the nerds of short stature and glasses who kept their heads down in the world's universities and colleges for years, waiting for their moment in the sun. Mao came, saw, conquered and died early enough for U.S.-style free trade economics to drive the country forward into the 21st century. In that respect, the Chairman's lusts gave life to China with his passing, the way Fidel's Spartan longevity did not for Cuba.

In Hong Kong, we sneeze and wheeze, our sinuses infected beyond repair. Pollutants drift downwind from up north because China industrializes, manufactures, synchronizes with the world to become the mother of all superpowers. Yet even our "freedoms of speech" absolve the Motherland; a recent government study confirms that the city's own carbon emissions are to blame for the state of our air ways.

Who knew? The one-time sleeping giant across the border already has gargantuan dams and shining highways to bolster and link the exploding urban centers. Maytag is replaced by Haier, Hollywood by Bamboo-Go-Lightly, freedom fries by naughty noodles. Steel mills will rise in Eastern hinterlands while American steel workers "retrain" for absent jobs. Britney Spears is welcome as long as she doesn't undress but Hilary Clinton must choose her words for entry. And the 2008 Olympics logo blazes across Tiananmen Square, a proud symbol and photo op for the masses. It's Free World *dim sum,* and China has an appetite for more, picking off from whichever cart suits her fancy.

Gently but firmly, as befits a responsible parent-state, China will strip this little city of our unnatural resources to aid in this endeavor. Canto-pop? Infotainment? Shop-till-you-flop? Sure. Rumblings of democracy? Reminders of Tiananmen? No way. Many in Hong Kong offer themselves up willingly, since those who protest are not the governing elite, not those who engage the world's ears and eyes with the promise of shiny lucre. They will negotiate and implement Beijing's diplomacy, as swiftly and with as little fuss as they can, so that the world will barely register protests for longer than a second in the global information gush.

But these are the political musings that befit the citizen of a nation state! Hong Kong is now a Chinese city, post-colonial perhaps, but hardly liberated. It once was, in the words of the journalist Richard Hughes, a "borrowed place" living on its "borrowed time." We've been self funding for a long time now, with our regulated and transparent stock exchange, a *laissez-faire* capitalist economy and a gambling appetite that fills the coffers of the Jockey Club, which in turn funds hospitals, schools and other socially necessary infrastructure. In fact, we've even recorded our history, and schoolchildren today are brought on field trips to a proud new museum where exhibits prove that yes, the Chinese roamed these shores long before the British arrived and will continue to do so now that they're finally gone.

If the gods are smiling on our people, as they did on Monkey, *laissez-faire* mothering will *laissez* us alone.

I am not a Chinese citizen, although ethnicity allows me to be. What I am is a Hong Kong *yan*, my gaze fixed on an evanescent home, trusting it will find form and footing somehow as a Chinese city. All I have to be is a writer from within, who can and must record this transit. *Sic transit gloria mundi.* May the pearl's luster not fade too soon.

Pop Goes the Idol

Why Hong Kong Can't Write or The William Hung Theory of Writing and Literature with Apologies to J.M. Coetzee

This essay is adapted from a pseudo-academic paper delivered at the University of Hong Kong, English Department Seminar, December 2004.

I have puzzled for some time over the absence of a "native literature" from my city. My three-year experience of compiling *City Voices,* an anthology of Hong Kong prose and poetry in English of the last fifty years, showed that while a fledgling literature has emerged, its evolution is slow compared to other colonial and post-colonial literatures, and its future precarious and uncertain. What proved a more significant ancillary discovery was that even Hong Kong Chinese writing, certainly more mature and evolved than that in English, receives minimal attention on the world's literary stage. Global economic realities dictate that translations of English literature into Chinese surpass the reverse, but it is almost frightening how little Hong Kong Chinese literature exists in English or any other translation.

Attendant to this is a lack of interest in literature generally in modern Hong Kong. There are hardly any publishers of serious local literature. Few academics write about or study the local literature that does exist. Our secondary schools barely teach English or Chinese Literature as subjects, never mind the home-grown offerings, and few students elect to take Literature in the public exams.

The teaching of "creative writing" exists in local schools and universities and has for some years, but this has as yet contributed little to a native literature. Perhaps in time, things could change, but we must wonder why it's taking so long.

Is it possible this lack of sustainable production and interest is, in fact, because Hong Kong simply can't write?

What a terrible question to confront for a Hong Kong native who has dedicated her life to the writing of serious fiction and essays, and the reading of literature. My city comprises an educated and sophisticated populace, literate in three plus languages. We have a middle class bourgeoisie which is typically a pre-condition for the arts to flourish. Other serious art forms emerge more readily, contribute to our culture and garner local and international recognition, most notably our independent films such as those by Wong Kar Wai.

If all the ingredients for the production of literature exist, the real question perhaps should be: Then why doesn't Hong Kong write? Is it because it can't or won't?

Here are three possible reasons. The first is the classic cliché, universally true but particularly applicable here: You can't make a lot of money as a writer, and especially so if you aspire to be "literary." Our pragmatic culture does not value the study of the humanities which requires, as literature does, analysis and often painful reflection on the truth of the human condition, which is a second reason our citizenry will shrug and say, why "cramp your brain muscles," it's not like you can change anything. After all, our history as a colonial people — and even our "post-colonial" state resembles the colonial, despite a less foreign ruling culture — is reason enough to downplay the pen in favor of keeping the master's sword at bay. But the real reason, the deep-rooted one that has long been there regardless of politics and the economy is this: *our parents simply won't let us.*

Hong Kong parents are famous, even infamous, for pushing their children towards the practical in life. You learn English, or these days, Putonghua because fluency will help you get a job, and not necessarily because of any love of either language. Likewise you get an MBA or a degree in engineering for reasons of survival, and not from a passionate desire to create enterprises or build bridges. As our city accumulated wealth, more opportunities emerged for young people to indulge their desire for sports, the arts or other such "trivial pursuits" as reading and writing. But the mandate remains: any life-long endeavor that meets "parental approval" is one that must have a practical outcome, i.e.: making a living. If we extrapolate from that to the culture at large, Hong Kong as the "parental authority" is unlikely to allow us to pursue an artistic, or more specifically, literary career.

In our electronic, audio-visual world, the arts and entertainment are increasingly linked. "Artistic" endeavors embody expectations of not just money, but the fame of television, movies, commercial sponsorships, even "Google searchability." Publishers are guaranteed success if they turn celebrities into "writers." *I am Jackie Chan,* the movie star's autobiography penned with a "co-author" (arguably the only author) likely sells more copies than all the books by Xi Xi, Louise Ho, Dung Kai-Cheung, Leung Ping-kwan and Agnes Lam combined. And a "real job," as a university academic as some of these real writers are, is acceptable if you must write.

Do we not write because we too much need that "parental approval"? I recall bumping into a former colleague, many years earlier, when I still had a "real job" in corporate life back before my first book was published. We had once been peers at the same company and friends in our twenties, but my work life took a detour in favor of a MFA in fiction, a degree which did little to advance or enhance my corporate career. He was now a managing director at a major multinational, while I a mere manager at another. On learning I was a serious writer, he looked puzzled for a moment, frowned, and then, in a tone of mock pity exclaimed, "Oh, so you still go for all that bohemian life!" I smiled, said nothing, and got the discount I needed now that he was a Very Important Person who could bestow such favors.

Where did his attitude come from? Does it signify a value system that cannot embrace artistic endeavors except to deride them as "bohemian," because his tone was clearly derisive. But what I prefer to recall is the younger man who poured his friends expensive champagne, appropriated from his father's liquor cabinet, back in what were arguably his "bohemian" days, before his hair was white and his face lined with worry over marketing, profits and the protection of his job when the layoffs eventually came.

In mulling over this question, I was struck by the example of a Hong Kong celebrity in what can loosely be termed "the arts" (and certainly, entertainment) who provides me a "theory" for the writing of our literature.

William Hung, whose fifteen minutes of fame since his appearance on "American Idol" in January, 2004, looks poised to linger awhile or at least as long as Asia is enamored of such fame. His CD "Inspiration" sold nearly 400 million copies; he has performed at several major concerts and is making a second movie. He has been widely interviewed by the media and, despite waning fame, is still a kind of superstar, especially on the internet. The University of Hong Kong recently hosted him as a speaker, an event that drew a crowd of over two hundred. Not bad for the geeky Chinese kid who was told by a scornful, if bewildered, "American Idol" judge that he "can't sing, can't dance, what do you want me to say?" but who is now singing and dancing his way to greater success. Since Hung might seem an odd digression in an inquiry about writing, let me also cite J.M. Coetzee, whose thoughts on literature (despite the artifice of the novel in which these appear) are, at the very least, difficult to ignore. *Isn't that what is most important about fiction: that it takes us out of ourselves, into other lives?* So says John, a character in Coetzee's latest novel, *Elizabeth Costello.*

So let us go then, you and I, guided by my instincts as a fiction writer, into another life, so that we might further unravel this literary puzzle about the city whence I hail.

Here's some "Hong Kong writing" which, if not by Hung himself, has been sanctioned by him and his handlers:

> Meet William Hung. A student at UC Berkeley, William studies Civil Engineering, but his dream is to make music his career. William has true talent, and has captured the hearts of Americans across the country who watched him sing and dance his heart out on Tuesday, January 27. Since his TV debut, William has gathered a large fan base. Nobody ceases to be amused by his comical dance moves and earnest rendition of "She Bangs". Because we respect William's true talent and comical ability, we have decided to create this fan club dedicated to William himself. (from www.williamhung.net — the official Website to William Hung a.k.a. Hong Kong's Ricky Martin)

Describing his abilities as both that of a comic and a "true talent" in musical performance, is intriguingly schizophrenic. American media has lauded, reviled and named his performances everything from "lovable" to "American Sambo" to "conceptually adventurous"; the latter, from *The New York Times* review of his "Zootopia" appearance at Madison Square Garden concludes thus: "for one exquisite, terrifying moment it seemed he might not leave the stage until he had shredded Ricky Martin's entire catalog." Ricky Martin, to date, has made no comment on his Hong Kong doppelganger. While American media might differ in their opinion of Hung's fame, on one thing they do seem to agree: William Hung is not a pop musical talent. Of his comedic ability, the jury is still divided; he appears to garner higher praise for "sincerity" and "honesty" than for any conscious comedic ability. "I already gave my best," Hung told the judges after his live audition was abruptly terminated. *"I have no regrets at all."*

What his American fame did ensure, much like Lee Lai-shan's Olympic windsurfing gold medal, was subsequent hero worship back "home," meaning in Hong Kong. Three months after his "American Idol" performance, he told the *South China Morning Post*: "I looked like an idiot up there. I want to be good, not something that people will laugh at. My singing wasn't horrible but my dancing really made it look silly. It's not like I'm a horrible singer who can't sing. But I don't have the consistency or the presentation skills that a good performer has." At that point, his parents encouraged his dreams of pop stardom, but in true Hong Kong parental fashion were pragmatic to a fault: "He's an easygoing guy and he'll just keep going," his mother is quoted as saying in the same interview. "Maybe he will have a long future in this business and maybe he won't. We'll see." After all, Hung is still a student with a future in civil engineering; his Berkeley professor says he's a B student who could be scoring A's.

Since looking "like an idiot," Hung has begun voice and performance coaching as a way of achieving his dream. His second movie, however, stars him in a comedy role, and he says that his honesty and belief in himself are the qualities that will keep him going. During his appearance at the University of Hong Kong, he told a cheering crowd, "If you believe in what you're doing, you will eventually succeed." He said this after being "almost dumbstruck" by a student who questioned him, in what one journalist called a "critical tone," as to what qualities he thought he had with which to live up to the role of a superstar. What the questioner perhaps failed to appreciate is that superstardom was visited upon Hung who appears not to have sought it in the first instance — he says his audition on "American Idol" was predicated on a whim — and whether or not he lives up to the role is irrelevant for one who already has achieved his fifteen minutes of superstardom, and more.

The William Hung story, like most public stories, has already turned into a kind of "reality fiction," and is a remarkable example of an artistic endeavor, Hong Kong style. Despite his accidental fame, some leap of faith drove the young man to that initial, musically suspect, performance. His family's karaoke hobby was apparently sufficient preparation for one who confessed on American national television that he had no professional training, a statement made with a seeming lack of irony. He says he has sung since he was a boy. Did he, at some point, want to study music and was denied by his parents? We will probably never know. The Hungs immigrated to California when he was eleven. Did young William never imagine that musical training, or a recognizable talent, might precede public performance? Or was he simply sold on the Hong Kong notion that music, even pop music, like all the arts, is merely a hobby, and that what makes a life is a career in civil engineering? Even Britney Spears, a mega-, not merely a super-star who, arguably, cannot sing without electronic enhancement, can at least dance; she was a Disney Mouseketeer, a form of professional training and recognition of talent in the pop cultural world.

While Hung's singing may not be "horrible," there is no denying that he was rhythmically and tonally off key. His story is preceded and paralleled by "I, Wing" of New Zealand, a considerably older Hong Kong émigré who records and markets her screeching "operatic" renditions of the Beatles and *Phantom of the Opera*. Like Hung, she appears to be entirely sincere and not even slightly ironic, earnest in her desire to succeed as a serious singer. Her fame, however, is less far reaching. Age is undoubtedly a factor, as is locale, although her website almost exploded from all the hits. She did however rate an animation appearance on the satiric TV cartoon show *South Park*. But like Hung, she continues to reap profits from her "artistic" enterprise.

Hung is likely to endure as a much bigger "Hong Kong phenomenon" than an American or even Asian-American one; his Asian fans are more enthusiastic than his American ones, he claims. He seems unconscious of Asian-American stereotyping and has been unfavorably compared to the Mickey Rooney character in *Breakfast at Tiffany's*, "complete with buck teeth, bad hair and bad accent." Nor does he seem sensitive to American race politics. "Hung is just a foreigner in this country trying to get an education," writes one African-American critic, "who can't know how being a talent show buffoon will affect his livelihood or the dignity of his countrymen." Yet the swooning legion of fans in Hong Kong, and Asia, who bombard the self-confessed virgin bachelor with proposals of marriage and who praise his "courage" and ability to make them feel good about themselves, mirrors local expectations *vis-à-vis* the arts, albeit explicitly commercial art: *here's one of our own who made it big abroad, never mind how, and now he's making tons of money for that "artistic expression" so we love him*. In fairness to Hung, he may yet turn into "the next big comedian," as his co-star Nancy Sit predicts. Even if he never gains acceptance as a "serious singer," a future as a civil engineer might not be his only option.

Regardless of what we think of Hung's talent, or lack thereof, it is difficult to deride his indomitable spirit, despite his curious self-image. His naïveté is, however, more troubling, because it stems from an ignorance of artistic standards and expectations that surely cross national boundaries, despite the American platform that launched him. Would William Hung have become a superstar in Hong Kong had he produced a music video of that same rendition of "She Bangs" and competed with the numerous, extremely earnest, talented local pop singers, not all of who need electronic enhancement? I have difficulty imagining one of our serious local performers promoting self parodies on a web site without the hint of a cringe, until the Hung phenomena, that is; having butchered the original, he now treats us to "She Clangs," a version of the Martin song as performed by a cartoon Hung with an animated cow. It puts me in mind of the Frank Marcus play, *The Killing of Sister George*, where the only role left for a has-been radio drama actress is that of a mooing cow. The despair depicted in that tragi-comedy is almost as bleak as Joseph Conrad's "the horror, the horror," first uttered from the heart of darkness of our human condition, only to be later parodied by Elmer Fudd, *the howwor, the howwor.*

What could we anticipate if our society more willingly read and contemplated Hong Kong and World Literature in greater measure? As astounding, amusing or tragic as Hung's success might eventually prove to be, in the world of pop art, no one questions commercial and financial success, and certainly, his parents appear content and approving of that success. Would they have been as forgiving or accepting if young William had insisted on the serious study of music, of honing what talent he might or might not have, of setting the bar higher than that of his home-alone karaoke hobby sessions? To study singing or creative writing is no guarantee of future success as a singer or writer, but what it will do is encourage questions and reflections, as well as instill a deeper understanding of what it takes to make art, including pop art. Most of all, ignorance and naïveté cannot prevail; initiating artistic endeavors may require a certain blind faith, but only critical self examination by the artist, as opposed to loud protestations of sincerity, will result in art and literature that enriches a culture.

So it is hard to write, or sing, in a fashion that is not just "good" but taps into the well of humanity, and that, perhaps, is the Hong Kong dilemma. There are no guarantees, no insurance policies to buy, no well-paid jobs at the end just because you work hard or have a dream or get a degree. It also takes true courage, by which I do not mean the temerity to make a fool of yourself on TV because you don't know any better, although even that instinct is not entirely misguided. Art and literature arise from genuine passion which is often the catalyst to make you a laughing-stock, or at worst, a miserable failure. One of China's great novels did not become a success till some forty years after the author's death; Cao Xueqin self-published a handful of copies of *The Dream of Red Chambers* in his lifetime and died a pauper. His parents more than likely did not approve of this "writing thing" he did.

Pragmatism is born of a desire for security. Should we let that desire overwhelm our literary culture? While teaching a creative writing workshop for English teachers at the Institute of Education, I was struck by one teacher's comment. We were reading some local poetry to serve as examples for the participants' own creative attempts. One woman appeared slightly perturbed at having to read any poems, especially those by local poets. She wanted to know why they needed to care about actual published poetry since wasn't this just an exercise in writing poems, which anyone can do, and after all, none of them need aspire to real poetry anyway? It was an unnerving moment. That an English secondary school teacher would so easily dismiss even the possibility of poetic expression as a desire did not made her much of a candidate to encourage the budding poets among her charges. More worrying was what she might consider necessary to teach her students in creative writing. Real poetry? Of course not. Whatever they wrote would be enough. There were examples of "poetry" on the classroom bulletin board: rhyme and abundant sentimentality were evident, but little else.

One man's story does not a culture make. Perhaps I demand too much of this phenomenon, which could easily go the way of the kiwi by next spring or whenever the next "superstar" appears. Yet Hung's impact, not just as a commercial success but as a role model for youth, is difficult to dismiss. He wishes to remain true to himself, to not give up his dream, to brush aside all negativity that surrounds any famous person (one fake news item reported that he committed suicide by overdosing on heroin, a stab, no doubt, at his innocent, good boy image). As admirable as these sentiments might seem on the surface, is such unwavering belief sufficient? Is it unnecessary to question the human condition through reading and writing literature, except to assert, like the English teacher, that writing is whatever we make of it?

We can envision, in this electronic age, the disappearance of books and literature into cyberspace. In that case, Hong Kong might be on the cutting edge, the precursor of things to come, of a culture that is utterly democratic in its artistic standards and where too much thought about endeavors that cannot be a financial success equals a waste of time. At a Hong Kong literary festival dinner some years prior, one financial sponsor raised her toast to "these writers, who must be fed, after all," generating much laughter. It was an odd, self-conscious, but unconsciously rude remark on the need to honor and support literary creation, as if writers should simply produce literature invisibly and not sully those who labor at "real jobs" with their distressing humanity. Are we all to be relegated to the fate of Ralph Ellison's "invisible" man or Alexander Solzhenitsyn's Ivan Denisovich? Hong Kong does not support writers with much by way of government funding, awards, fellowships or residencies; our budding Eileen Changs or Gao Xinjians or Ha Jins might fare better if they head for Hollywood and play the clown, because then they might win respect back home.

Towards the end of *Elizabeth Costello* — the title names the protagonist, an aging novelist of international renown who could be read as Coetzee's doppelganger — Costello is "at the gate" of the end of her life's journey where she must write a statement of beliefs and face her own panel of judges. Her thoughts turn into a dark meditation on her writing life in which she says:

> And if that is a cliché too — being a professional, playing one's part — then let it be a cliché. What entitles her to shudder at clichés when everyone else seems to embrace them, live by them?
>
> It is the same with the business of belief. I believe in the irrepressible human spirit: that is what she should have told her judges. That would have got her past them, and with foot-stamping applause too. I believe that all humankind is one. Everyone else seems to believe it, believe in

it. Even she believes in it, now and then, when the mood takes her. Why can she not, just for once, pretend?

When she was young, in a world now lost and gone, one came across people who still believed in art, or at least in the artist, who tried to follow in the footsteps of the great masters . . . Has she carried that childish faith into her late years and beyond: faith in the artist and his truth?

Her first inclination would be to say no. Her books certainly evince no faith in art . . . her books teach nothing, preach nothing; they merely spell out, as clearly as they can, how people lived in a certain time and place. More modestly put, they spell out how one person lived, one among billions: the person whom she, to herself, calls she, and whom others call Elizabeth Costello. If, in the end, she believes in her books themselves more than she believes in that person, it is belief only in the sense that a carpenter believes in a sturdy table or a cooper in a stout barrel. Her books are, she believes, better put together than she is.

So ends this modest inquiry of one puzzled soul, with apologies to a literary giant in whose shadow I continue to find solace. This digression into William Hung's reality fiction was necessary, I believe, because his story exemplifies how people lived in a certain time and place known as Hong Kong today. He is a product of our culture, and is instructive for the creative urge in others from this same world.

As for our native literature, all I might have established is that it is still risky to write here, now, to investigate uncertainties, surrounded as we are by those of such unwavering faith. A long time ago, I learned to disregard parental and societal disapproval, given my quixotic quest to be a writer. I can't be sure, even now, whether I do aspiring young writers a service or disservice by encouraging their endeavors. All I know is that I do encourage because literature is a passion that must somehow find a voice.

I feel a peculiar kinship with young William, who made his world-famous debut on my fiftieth birthday. To take a page from the William Hung playbook: have I, as a writer, "already given my best"? Oh, I hope not, I sincerely hope not, because the only reason for continued artistic expression is to keep surpassing yourself. But on his second point, I partially agree with this irrepressible human spirit, which is that if I had my writing life to do over again, I would do it again, and about that, I too have few, but not *no* regrets.

in the city-village

the cuckoo is on the mulberry-tree;
her young go astray;
but good folk, gentle folk —
their ways are righteous.
their ways are righteous,
their thoughts constrained.

from **"Blessings on Gentle Folk" The Book of Songs** *(nr 165)*
translated by Arthur Waley

Random Reality Show

Ask a British lady who could lunch back in the sixties and she might recall this tune on air: *Good morning, good morning / It's great to stay up late / Good morning, good morning / To you how do, how do you do?* Bouncy, silly, happy. This old show tune was the theme song for a radio program "Housewife's Choice." It puzzled me whenever I heard it as a child, because I could not imagine who in Hong Kong would "stay up late" to listen to such a program.

This is a city of random reality. *Your Hong Kong is not my Hong Kong*, we seem to say to each other in this small space we share with such civility. Why is it possible for us to be so separate even as we bump elbows everywhere we turn? Perhaps a reality check, as I travel through my city districts will tell, a *Truman Show* journey through life as it has been and continues to be.

Kowloon Motor Bus number 208 still goes to Broadcast Drive, as it did when I lived there in the late seventies, in one of my only Hong Kong residences which I also partially owned. Most of my other homes were rentals. My one-bedroom was enormous at 700 sq. ft. for a solo woman, divorced, who traveled frequently for business and pleasure. Next door, in a slightly larger flat whose verandah was at right angle to mine, lived five young girls and their parents. *Jie jie, jie jie,* the girls chanted in unison, once they realized this "big sister" would occasionally stick her head out from behind the curtains and say hello. I had a piano in my bedroom next to a Scandinavian double bed, no living room furniture, and a wooden dining table with two chairs. There was also a built-in wardrobe and dresser, a two-ring burner in the kitchen and a washer-dryer in the huge bathroom with a tub I never filled, preferring showers. A major problem was plumbing. The kitchen sink occasionally backed up with the refuse from above (this was the seventh floor of a twelve-story building), until I sealed off my drains against the flow, and they gurgled contentedly ever after.

It was an odd time to live alone with a mortgage and airline benefits. All my local friends were either single and living with their parents, or married and living either in their own flats or with parents. No one had space, except one or two very wealthy friends whose family homes included three-car garages, private entrances for the returned graduate's flat and money to spare for "investments" in jewelry or stocks until the right husband came along to provide, or the right wife showed up to legitimize moving out. By contrast, my cross-cultural and expatriate friends included families, couples, divorced "singles" as well as singles from several countries who lived in huge, company-paid flats with maids (plus access to corporate launches, holiday homes and all the other perks). Even those without expatriate benefits lived quite differently from most locals.

But Broadcast Drive was a good choice for a born-again local like me. The street is named for its function, because all the television and radio station used to be located on this hillside horseshoe at the foot of the Lion Rock tunnel. My parents lived within a ten-minute walk up a higher hill slightly north, yet these two hilly locales were, literally, night and day. Their suburban neighborhood was a pretender to exclusivity, where middle and upper middle class civil servants, bank employees, and other respectable business and professional people raised children to become like them, or so they hoped. The bus was rarely full because everyone had a car; even taxis hesitated to circle the block, wasting petrol when, more often than not, they could not get a fare. By early evening, the streets were empty because all decent folks were home at the table where a soup, two *soongs* of meat or seafood or tofu, and vegetables, would be served hot, with steaming white rice. Mother or grandma prepared this daily feast, usually with the help of a servant, and the Hong Kong version of the extended nuclear family would sit down to dine.

Mine was the upstart neighborhood, where too many buildings with small flats went up too quickly, or so people said. Management at my building, unlike that at my parents', rarely paid attention to who came and went because too many people did. To residents in Kowloon Tong, the district which embraced both our neighborhoods, Broadcast Drive brought an unwelcome *jaap* character of shift workers, flight attendants (we were close to Kai Tak International), entertainment industry folks pretending to be respectable, and families striving to be more middle class than they really were. Fewer homes had maids.

Ergo, me. I slotted right in. The bus was a necessity and there were always taxis, night and day.

Sixty-five to 70% of my "very good salary" (around HK$3,500 a month, roughly what a domestic helper makes thirty year later) went towards half my mortgage; my parents paid the other half. Utilities, rates, taxes and living expenses ate up the rest. Luckily, men still paid restaurant and bar bills back then which meant that as long as I dated, I ate and drank better than I earned. When I didn't date because I had a novel chapter or story to finish, food was basic. Fortunately, I was a runner, doing six miles each morning after writing and before work, so health was on the side of my weird, "glocalized"-before-it-was-fashionable existence. No one, except crazy foreigners — like my American marathons-around-the-world boyfriend — ran.

Was this really a Hong Kong life? Once during those days, on a flight to Bahrain, I sat next to a dark-skinned Hong Kong Chinese woman. She was slightly older than me and also divorced. "I love to travel on business," she said. "You meet so many men." It was discomfiting, that echo of my life. I was perpetually tanned, more or less had a lover in every port, but could not articulate the meaning of home. Once during those days, grapevine whispers were repeated back to me, about how I went to bars alone. The gossip was a local Chinese woman who didn't even know me personally. How startling that my strange existence proved such a fascinating subject. There are many Hong Kong's someone like me could elect to live, but clearly, my Hong Kong was nothing like hers.

Now, on an early summer afternoon, I head towards an outdoor exhibit at Shek Kip Mei commissioned by the Arts Development Council. The photographer has spent two years shooting the last residents in this public housing estate. His photos are a stark reminder of the elderly, often alone, in our city today. In Christmas of 1953, a fire devastated the squatter huts on the hillsides of this district, leaving some 50,000 homeless. The government soon rebuilt public housing in the area, constructing inelegantly cold but space-efficient concrete blocks. These blocks are empty now, scheduled for demolition, a history our city tries to eradicate of formerly impoverished lives. Yet the photo exhibit courts remembrance: these were our homes and families, even if the young ones fled, the silent images say. This was our reality.

Once upon a time, when I was a teenage Girl Guide, I had a friend whom I will call Veronica. She was my idol: a whiz at lighting campfires, pitching tents, flinging lifelines across the school yard in our rope throwing exercises. Her uniform was always starched and ironed, her shoes shined, her yellow tie perfectly knotted, lanyard hooked in place at the belt. She occasionally visited my home, and my mother was always happy to welcome this well-mannered and neat older girl, someone she approved of as her daughter's companion.

But in the six years I knew her, I only visited her home once.

It was almost summer, if I recall correctly, and I was around fourteen or so. We had been at our weekly Guides meeting and, as was our habit, we lingered afterwards into the late afternoon, often to take walks in the city over a soft drink or ice cream, chattering away about the politics of our group, the 19th Kowloon Company, because this was the thing that most occupied the hours outside of school. We had decided to go somewhere which was near where Veronica lived. *Come home with me a moment,* she said, and I agreed.

That was when I first realized she lived in a public housing block. It was one of the old style blocks, like Shek Kip Mei. If there was a lift, I don't remember it. What I do recall was walking down a long open air walkway on a high floor, and stopping at a metal door that led into an empty flat, one that was only slightly larger than the bedroom I shared with my two sisters. Veronica, I knew, had siblings, parents and even a grandparent with whom she lived. The communal bathroom and kitchen were somewhere else on the floor.

We stayed a few minutes while she dropped off her stuff. The shock of encountering her reality stayed with me for a long time afterwards.

In my government-subsidized public school, many of my schoolmates were middle class, and quite a few were from wealthy families. Although I was aware that some of my classmates were less well off — the scholarship girls for instance — it had not dawned on me till then that Veronica was any different from me. She did not mention having to work after school, as some girls did. Nor did she ever look unwashed or unkempt, as one of the scholarship girls did. I was not a stranger to my city's poverty. My mother regularly made my sister and I go with her to the Little Sisters of the Poor, a charitable institution for the aged, on her visiting rounds where she handed out sympathy and cash. Also, I had been in the Legion of Mary in the lower forms, and part of our duties involved visiting the poor and elderly in *tong laus,* the low rise Chinese-style buildings without lifts which were often old and badly lit. My parents and the Hong Kong government spoke of public housing as a good thing, a sign of progress. Even though the Shek Kip Mei fire happened before I was born, in my youth, hillside squatters were still a reality as were the many beggars in the streets.

But Veronica's home, bereft of parental presence, was the cold reality of a latchkey kid before the term came into being. Her life suddenly confounded me: no one, I thought, should have to live with so little material well being. Veronica was not given to complaints. I am sure it was just home to her, and the fact that my home, and those of many of her classmates, might be larger, more luxurious or comfortable was beside the point. We are who we are, regardless.

When I fast forward to the post-handover, twenty-first century city, I see fragments of my former reality everywhere, and the way I used to live is more commonplace than not.

Our families are fracturing, sociologists say. So many of us dine alone on a regular basis. Children leave home and do not return, because their fathers, mothers, siblings and other relatives do likewise. Latchkey children are a long-standing phenomenon because both parents had to work in a city that once was poor. Now both parents work because women from elsewhere in Asia tend to their children and household chores. Young boys and girls cling to Filipino nannies who hug them when their parents cannot. Will a generation of Hong Kong boys seek out Filipino wives in memory of their *ayi's?* Will a generation of Hong Kong girls embrace unmarried life in solidarity with their mothers, abandoned for cross-border "little wives"? Will a generation of young professionals deem the indentured servitude of foreign domestic helpers their birthright, and complain of "ingratitude" when such workers demand more humane working conditions and higher pay?

At Lok Fu, one of the early modern style public housing estate with better facilities than Shek Kip Mei, an Indonesian domestic helps an elderly Chinese man down the stairs to the market square. This is his morning walk, alone with a woman who does not speak his language as a native tongue. On any given day, you will see several such scenarios repeated around the city, in moderate to low-income neighborhoods, and not just the wealthy ones. On Chinese talk radio, thirty- and forty-something talk show hosts complain of the new breed of twenty-somethings who, on getting a first job out of school, do not give 50% of their income to their parents — horrors! — as they, the older generation did. The much-heralded "Asian values" that honor family and filial duty are under threat. Globalized values are creeping in, creating an uncomfortable similarity in neighborhoods once distinguishable by social class.

Space remains an issue. Renovation is recreational activity in this city. Today, from my suburban rooftop under the Lion Rock, a panorama of bamboo scaffolding grace the buildings around me. We whitewash and paint, replace old pipes with new, pull apart no-longer fashionable décor to be replaced by that which is in vogue. Our spaces are in constant motion. Our daylight songs are punctuated by the jackhammers' refrain.

Here are the districts of my life in this city: Tsimshatsui by the harbor that used to be a mile wide at its narrowest span; Shatin of the paddy fields and train carriages; Sai Kung, in a tiny village, remote, overlooking a pristine bay; Kowloon Tong of elegant pre-war homes turned love motels, surrounded by trees and privacy; Causeway Bay of shopping, the city's first Japanese department store and a view of the Royal Yacht Club and typhoon shelter; Mid Levels of mosquitoes, narrow streets, noisy buses and overpriced flats. The last home I lived in during my former corporate work life was in Sheung Wan when it was quiet at night and not yet quite SOHO, in an Aberdeen Street *tong lau*. This former office of a jewelry company turned residential flat was florescent-lit with cold, tile flooring. I shared it with a family of geckos that nested on the water heater in winter and large hairy spiders that crawled up the drains of the shower in summer. I slept on two tatami mats without a mattress and filled the 370 sq. ft. studio with the remains of my second divorce. There was no washer-dryer (a laundry was next door), but there was a piano. These are the things we transport in various forms through the years of a city that is home.

In *Coming Home*, a 2003 film directed by Peter Chan Ho-sun, Eric Tsang plays an ex-cop who brings his young son "home" to a deserted compound, the former police residential quarters on Aberdeen Street, opposite where I lived. The boy sees a young girl about his age who keeps appearing and disappearing, in much the way the ghost girls do in Stephen King's *The Shining*. The only other residents appear to be an elderly man and a Chinese herbal doctor and his wife; she turns out to be the wife's corpse the doctor has preserved — he has strangled her to "save" her — sure that she will resurrect soon. When the ex-cop stumbles upon this bizarre scenario, the doctor imprisons him, forcing him to witness the preparations for the resurrection. Meanwhile, the young son is left to fend for himself, and follows his ghost girl playmate into her past, looking for a path to something that feels like "home."

We stumble down roads less or more traveled, searching for a tangible space, imagining an ideal room, believing that home will keep us safe. My Aberdeen Street flat was just below the square where the hungry ghosts festivities erupted each summer, a colorful pageantry outside the neighborhood district office on Staunton of ritual offerings, re-enactments, musical programs. Even the dead return to roam the earth, alighting around my former homestead, turning their nosy gazes on occupied and vacant flats, expecting us to allow them space for their peregrinations. The square is silent now, having fallen prey to property development and the encroaching boundaries of SOHO, providing homes for the new young elite. Nightlife disrupts ghost life, and the hungry dead roam elsewhere each August.

Reality is more than random or relative. It has much to do with the edge of desires and dreams. My family approved my first marriage, disapproved the divorce, disapproved the second marriage and were resigned to that divorce when it happened. They long ago gave up on the idea of grandchildren from my lineage. Do we choose a way to live that sets us apart because the existing environment will not contain us, or do we stumble into homes and districts and lives because fate leads us where she will?

I can't imagine living anywhere but Hong Kong, say friends and relatives who have alternatives if they choose. One Hong Kong Chinese friend shifts from a larger space on one hilltop on the island to another further west, her new sanctuary against China and the world. She functions bi-lingually, fluently, a successful entrepreneur who does not read Chinese although you would never know it, and who keeps all trips into the Mainland deliberately short. Another reclaims space in her North Point family home after her mother's death; she has yet to travel beyond our shores although she promises she will visit me someplace else one day. Meanwhile, my uncle and aunt have never lived anywhere but Kowloon since their arrival years ago from Indonesia, and are settled now in Tsimshatsui. Convenient for the trains to Shenzhen for my aunt, and an easy transit to the airport for my uncle. My sister who surfs will probably never leave her beachfront village house on the south side of the island. The poet and critic Ya Se (Leung Ping-kwan) documented his move to Tuen Mun in a film. It was drastic, this move to the rural outback, after years of living in town. His relocation coincided with the handover and was a poignant comment on the times.

One friend, having returned years ago, divorced, after ten years in America, remarried after living alone in a remote village in the New Territories and found solace above the waterfront both west and east of Central. Her story is prescient: the building she and her husband live in, an older, low building along the hillside, is slated for development. All around her, old buildings have succumbed to development demolition, scattering long-time residents out of the fractured neighborhoods. The new buildings are taller, smarter, trendier, poking into our hillsides like so many skinny toothpicks, housing flats that are more hotel-homes than homes, offering profitable temporary abodes for globalized citizens, who could as easily live here, there, and everywhere.

In this city ruled by real estate, where women recite the price per square foot the way they once quoted the price per catty of market vegetables each morning, do districts and spaces take on greater significance? Photographers fill numerous volumes for libraries and coffee tables with shots of every corner of this city. What little we write of "our town" is eclipsed by these photos that paint hundreds of thousands of words for the world. *Look-see,* these pictures seem to say. *Locate your Hong Kong, it's here somewhere.*

The Truman Show, a 1998 film by the Australian director Peter Weir, is a visionary parody of the reality TV explosion that has hit global airwaves in recent years. Truman Burbank is a character on a 24-7 television program that has broadcast his life since birth. He grows up on a studio set that is called the town of Seahaven, surrounded by "family," "friends" and an entire "society," all played by actors. His life is a fictional creation, scripted by the megalomaniac director Christof. But Truman thinks this is reality, and so it is, until one day when things go awry and he begins to question his concocted "reality," which is how the story commences.

Aren't we all the stars of our own Truman Shows? What else accounts for this fascination with reality TV, with the constant jabber broadcast on board buses, trains and planes around and from this city? Why else the well worn cliché: truth is stranger than fiction?

During my cross-harbor ride on bus number 103 from Junction Road to Bonham Road, I watch Roadshow on bus TV. "When I first started performing," says an aspiring Canto-pop singer, "I wasn't accustomed to all the media attention. Now it's just life." He is a *leang jai,* interchangeable with all the other "beautiful boys" and girls globally who bare their earnest hearts on screen. Singers, dancers, actors, writers, musicians, visual artists — performers one and all — sharing their experiences and emotional responses, none of which are trivial, at least not to them. The media space-time continuum is reality, whether or not anyone watches, listens, remembers or cares. We confront our reality minute by minute, in text and instant messages. *Are you there, are you real,* we seem to be asking underneath all the chatter. *Or will you vanish when I switch off my device, the one connecting me to the world?*

It is increasingly difficult to locate a Hong Kong for life. Space remains an issue, less because of property prices but more because it vanishes and transforms at the speed of global desire. "Goods Of Desire," a successful local brand of designer household items, plays off its blasphemous acronym GOD. Our city's spirit has become a mischievous minor god, zapping this space when it feels out of date, crowning yet another for a moment in time, disrupting the universe we know. Our harbor may eventually enjoy only a fictive existence, one archived in the realm of historic memory; Queen's Pier has launched its last boat and is to be demolished so that yet more reclamation can raise highways from the sea, further shrinking the already shrunken waterway.

Qing wen, a young, fashionable, Mainland woman asked me at 11:30 last night, how do I get to Lan Kwai Fong? We were standing a few yards away from the center of the nightlife district on the slope above. It was midweek on a warm spring night. The bars and restaurants were noisy with revelers and would be for several more hours. This young tourist from up north wants the Hong Kong she's heard of, which is not the former British colony or shopping paradise (in fact, of late, Chinese tourists have reported retailers who have cheated them with fake goods). The Hong Kong that looms large for this young, hip border crosser is "California," "Beirut," "Insomnia," "Haven" or any of numerous other packed venues that serve as party central, where she and her girlfriend will hook up with revelers from someplace else, here in their Hong Kong of desire. I pointed behind me. There, I said, is *Laan Gwaai Fong,* inflecting in her tones, Putonghua. She smiled, thanked me, and ran up the hill as I headed downhill into the depths of the subway.

Less than five years earlier, Lan Kwai Fong on a similar night was deserted, thanks to S.A.R.S. and a faltering economy. How quickly we recover to renovate and reclaim the spaces of this city. How quickly, too, can we now forget the way we once were.

In *The Global Soul,* Pico Iyer writes of visiting an English school friend working in Hong Kong who lives in a hermetically sealed tower of expatriation where he functions 24-7 without ever leaving the complex. There is an instant superficiality about such a "global" experience, despite its very real existence, because it eradicates the meaning of the tangible, actual city. We can point to an earlier era of expatriate life in Hong Kong which fostered exclusive addresses on the Peak, high above the natives, or on the inaccessible south side, where large homes luxuriate in views of uninterrupted horizons. These are the same addresses the Mainland's *nouveau riche* now vie to acquire.

Yet as I meander from Sai Wan Ho at the eastern side of Hong Kong island to Mei Foo Sun Chuen in northwest Kowloon peninsula, or from Siu Hong in the far west of the New Territories to Chai Wan at the eastern end of Hong Kong island, I am not sure if those realities are not similarly as insular. There is a 7-11 or K Mart convenience store in every district, a Giordano or Bossini clothing retail outlet in every shopping mall, a Wing Wah or St. Honore cake shop in every MTR or KCR station. You need never leave your district to experience a Hong Kong that is much like the one an hour's journey away, even on the small outlying islands of Peng Chau, Lamma or Cheung Chau. Visitors to the U.S. sometimes complain of the sameness of the landscape across a gigantic, Macdonalized nation. I might say the same of this tiny, glocalized city, Hong Kong.

These are the districts I walk through when the postmodern glocalized city is too much. The heart of Yaumati, between the highway hugging the waterfront and the incessant honking horns of Nathan Road. On Temple Street as sunset rolls in, before all the hawkers for the night market have arrived, the intrepid and hungriest early birds already display their wares. The minutiae of daily life — AA batteries, packets of underwear, nail clippers — line up parallel to doorway restaurants serving curried squid balls, stewed tripe, rice porridge and noodles. In the Tsimshatsui network of streets that cuts across Nathan Road, as well as those parallel to it, east and west of Chungking Mansions and the Mosque, shopkeepers entice visitors in the babble of Babel's tongues, before that tower fell. Indian tailors make men and ladies suits in half a day or less; look-alike Shanghai Tang nouveau Chinese fashions sell for a quarter of the price of the genuine article; embroidered linen tablecloths, placemats and napkins — these echo the former "authentic Hong Kong" tourist experience that once made the city a shopper's paradise, unlike the authentic European designer brands on Nathan Road that today's Mainland tourists crave.

Wanchai's *agora* is a day to night paradox. By day a residential and commercial district, the place to go for computer goods and home improvements, by night a throwback to the Orientalist pleasure dome where girls from the wrong tracks desperately seek men from the right side who are slumming for a night or more with money to burn. How is it that Suzie Wong's ghost haunts us still, metamorphosed into Filipino, Thai, Vietnamese sex workers? A nod though to 21st century "Wanch," as the expats call it, because red lights co-exist with the flashing lights of happy hours and ladies' nights, a non-trendy alternative to Lan Kwai Fong. The Wanch, perhaps better called the Raunch, where to be seen is to be pissed or picked up, with no pretensions to cultural commentary.

To wander this city is to wonder. Why does Lai Chi Kok, literally "lychee corner" have no lychee trees, although several other species are planted there? What did Mr. Wylie do to deserve his particular road, the narrow link for two wider, busier thoroughfares, the locale of the girl guides headquarters, several in-town country clubs, a hospital? Wylie Road was my favorite teenage walkabout, because it was quiet, green, other worldly, just long enough a city hike to feel vigorous, just short enough not to lose precious time before or after girl guide meetings. How did Kowloon City manage to preserve its magnificent banyan for as long as it did, while planes swooped around the air above it? Are butterfly lovers more than myth since butterflies abound in urban concrete, a delicate miracle nature presents us with remarkable consistency?

On a weekday afternoon, I tried to locate the point on the vertical axis from where I once had access to the world. Chater House in Central has replaced Swire House, which for years housed the head office of Cathay Pacific Airways, my one-time employer. For a few years in the late seventies, I went to work each morning at my little office on the fifth floor, dreaming of the world beyond. The new structure is neither remarkable nor overpowering; 137 meters high — a skinny oblong gift wrapped in a glass and steel rectangular box — it is a white dazzle indoors where the marble is very, very slippery and global labels very, very there. The price tag of progress is everywhere evident in this "Emporis Building," the group it belongs to that claims "we index the world." To index is to point or indicate. It also means to move so that "a specific operation will be repeated at definite intervals of space." An "emporis" then, this fictive globalist word stolen from emporium — marketplace, trading space — where desire is bought and sold. Swire House, an equally unremarkable building if not for my personal acquaintance with it, has disappeared from view. Slippery steps now bring you to the world, neatly boxed in a tower that resembles hundreds of others across the seven seas.

Perhaps for a young city like this, preserving space is a random reality, a right-time-right-money-luck-of-the-draw moment that stays demolition. Our vision must be focused, distracted as we are by too many flashing neon lights and the deaths and resurrections of too many buildings. Yesterday, a pre-war two-story house in this city was just a home. Tomorrow it might be the last surviving example of a rare architecture. Archeologists unearth shards of ancient buildings, pieces of tools, pots and pans, and sometimes even entire households, preserved by time, allowing us a glimpse into the way we humans used to live and work. Who can visit judgment on the history we make except History itself? Your Hong Kong may not be my Hong Kong but which Hong Kong will the world remember?

In the same essay about his trip to my town, Iyer says that his friend "works — more and more of us do — in an accelerating world, for which the ideal base of operations was this international Home Page of a city." In less than twenty years of cyber reality, web space can already command a price per virtual square meter. Domains are dominated and desired, YouTube houses you in your own virtual TV screen, Google gallops the only globe that matters in this faster-than-a-speeding-mouse era of human existence.

My friend Veronica disappeared from my life a long time ago. Despite a thriving alumni network, all attempts to locate her have failed. Perhaps, as a mutual friend says, she does not wish to be located. She remains a persistent memory, however, a recognition of the random reality of fate that places you here, her there, and others elsewhere on the plane of existence.

And choosy housewives of yore still warble: *How do,* indeed, *how do you do?*

In these our curious times, we may as well sing of virtual reality, just as random and real as the footprint my city makes on this earth.

WHITE LABEL

"Here," says the taxi driver, as he hands me my change, a receipt and a card, "call us fifteen minutes before you need a car. We give 15% discounts and only charge one-way on the tunnels." A cell phone number in large print is the only information on the white blankness. Affixed to his dashboard are a PDA and cell phone, both of which appear wirelessly connected to the headphone and mike around his head and face. On the seat beside him is another cell phone, one he has used manually twice during the ride, a harrowing twenty-five-minute journey in Kowloon on a Sunday evening, fraught with this mobile enterprise. He is a dispatch center, locating rides for customers wishing to cross the harbor or travel in or out of the New Territories *(anyone out there for Pokfulam to La Salle Road via the Western tunnel?)*, as well as an information bank, directing drivers who find themselves in unfamiliar territory *(get off Castle Peak highway at exit ___ and then find ___, you're five minutes away)*. No thanks, I think, as I take the card and my packages out of his vehicle, grateful to be alive.

He was the model driver in every other way. His vehicle was first in line at a legal taxi stand in Tsimshatsui which was where I boarded. He knew exactly where I needed to go, checked regarding the turn off point, and took the shortest route possible. The car was clean, he was courteous, even apologetic for his noisy phone conversation to a fellow driver. Most of all, he was an excellent driver, sure of himself, fast but not over the speed limit, aware of the traffic around him. He changed lanes safely, did not get into road-rage wars with other drivers as some drivers will, did not poke around uncertainly like the ones who clearly do not know their way, or, for that matter, how to drive with confidence. And at a time where there is almost always a surplus of taxis who have to compete with an excellent mass transit system of minibuses, buses, trains and subways, isn't he a smart entrepreneur, technologically advanced, simply trying to make a little extra, right in keeping with our pragmatic money culture that bucks the system when the system doesn't earn you a decent enough living? Isn't that the promise of the globalized world of electronic mobility, that the individual is king of his survival and success?

There is precedence. In my childhood, every one had a "white label" license plate private-public car to call for longer or regular rides, to transport groups of students when school buses did not yet exist. These were cheaper than the "red label" un-metered public cars (usually a burgundy Mercedes) that you could call or hail in the streets, more expensive than a taxi, but the fare negotiable depending on the moment. Taxis were metered to a fixed tariff. The red labels have long since disappeared, although white labels persist, white being the color of private car license plates and the origin of that name. But I long ago gave up my white label car in favor of my regular taxi, because taxis are cheaper, more plentiful, and if my usual driver is unavailable, he will find me another. If for some reason I cannot reach him, the taxi company he works for can page another driver.

Anyone who has ever arrived at the airport and gone to the taxi line knows this to be true: there is *always* a taxi for any part of the city, the lines snaking way beyond the entrance. The drivers wait, and wait, and wait, often for hours, just as they do at the official ranks of the Kowloon Canton Railway. How wonderful, visitors to our city say, as they bypass the taxis for other forms of public or private transport. Meanwhile, taxi drivers juggle a precarious livelihood. Little wonder my erstwhile driver of the mobile office circumvents the system. He is one of many who ply the long distance trade, which is particularly lucrative late at night after the MTR and KCR have closed, and the cross harbor tunnel buses run on a reduced schedule.

But this is *jing seung,* we say, "normal" or really, *the way things have to be.*

Dewars White Label used to be my drink of choice. I could down six or more in a night with no ill effects. I did this often as a young woman, juggling drinks and dates with the greed for life that youth considers *jing seung.* Others overdose on climbing corporate ladders, making a mint in property or shares, holding lavish weddings, consuming designer brands and other such "necessities," as well as having more and more babies in a city that is bursting with an overload of people, while all around our world, discarded babies wail.

The night I decided to leave my first husband, it was early autumn in Sai Kung. We were slumming, or so the beautiful people would call my life, because

I was university educated and could have lived better, and he was a U.K. *gwailo.* In our colony, the white man was king, his burden notwithstanding.

Dinner, which I dutifully cooked after work, having first stopped on the way home to shop at the wet market, was ready. I was twenty-three, too absurdly young to be married over a year, nursing a beer. Dinner was ready and turning cold as it had on many evenings. My husband, I knew, was at one of his pubs, the way he was pretty much every day as his business slowed, dwindled, evaporated. This was not news; shortly after we announced our engagement, he was let go from his job so this fit the pattern. I was primary breadwinner, maid, cook, as well as bookkeeper and administrator for his business in addition to my full-time job.

You might say I married badly, or foolishly, or too young, all of which was true. But in truth, I also married out of pride, because life as a college student in America had been a dream that ended when homecoming was not a choice. I could not replicate life abroad, of evenings spent trawling the bars of independence, blowing my waitressing tips on drinks and cigarettes, arguing about books and philosophy, being bohemian. A university graduate in Hong Kong of the early seventies comes home to stay. I broke out, shacked up with the first *gwailo* boyfriend that crossed my path and before I knew it, married to regain a modicum of respectability. Naturally, I got a good job because what choice was there in the face of your family's sacrifice?

My *gwailo* working class husband, on the other hand, married well.

So there it was, early autumn, my extramarital affair lurking in the shadows, and a dinner going cold. All we had was beer in the fridge. A pre-marital memory: Dewars and soda, on the rocks, lined up two on the bar, bought for me by some man hoping to get lucky, hoping to *make his day,* and night.

I wanted a scotch. Craved it. It was past eight and Sai Kung was a long way from the city. Even if I drove, we couldn't afford a car, and our only vehicle was my husband's motorbike which he had. Even if I made it into the city, there were no bars I could comfortably go to alone. Besides, the only ones I knew were where he drank, the last places I wanted to go.

I did the next best thing: hopped on public transport and headed to the airport bar.

There used to be a bar which has disappeared along with that airport. It was quiet there and the bartender poured me White Label. I sat and drank, and drank, even though it was a work night, because I couldn't feel a thing and knew that morning would be just another rude awakening. That was *jing seung.*

There is a word, "blackface," that recalls a peculiar racial imbalance in America. African American performers blackened their dark skin and painted white lips and eyes, clown faces, to sing and dance, entertaining white America. My city should have a word, "whiteface," for the blanching pallor which is the cross-cultural misstep of my first marriage. He was a good man, and I loved him once as he loved me, but in the Hong Kong of aspirations, where life is about the bounty of money and status, where to be even moderately privileged means to repay your debt to society by the "correct" choice of lifestyle, there was no room for two foolish young things, intoxicated by spirits and dreams of an alternate universe, far out in the countryside of Sai Kung.

My dreams were modest: enough money for taxis to and from Sai Kung; the opportunity to advance in a career if I worked hard; a husband who would be a partner for life. That October, as I drank into the night, I knew that all the intellectual excuses I could make for my home city did not mean a thing. There was no rightness or wrongness about the racial injustices of our colonial life, anymore than there is an absolute answer to why our Chinese sovereign culture is now the dominant elite. What if Brittania hadn't ruled the waves? There would have been no Hong Kong, my parents would never have met, I would not have been born and certainly not married to a British national who could live and work here by virtue of his race and not his qualifications. And I would not be seated at the Kai Tak airport bar, around midnight in autumn, circa 1976, a memory, evanescent like the city that used to be.

It is all about "aspiration," the desire Hong Kong seems to have to earn more and more in order to do more and more and even more. It is the modern global phenomenon, probably, but this city embraces it, lives and breathes it, accelerates life to a manic pace as if afraid of being left behind. After my first marriage ended, I too was infected by that virus of desire and enterprise. *Do the Hustle* was a popular song that had just peaked, an energetic refrain.

My home today is in a tiny village in the far northeastern corner of New York State. The leaves flame in autumn along my road. It is quiet here, where I look out onto woods and empty land, the lake in the distance. Is this my reward for having given into the hustle of Hong Kong life, the neverending drama of enterprise, of chasing desire to the ends of the known world?

If I had children, would I tell them to chase that virus? Or would I say, take a load off, relax, and when they were old enough, pour them a scotch and soda, the way my father once did for me, from the bottle of White Label that is ever present, in whatever space I call home.

Door

I slip in. I slip out. Tonight, Karissa is my Muse, the jazz guitarist who leads her band. The all-Hong Kong trio performs jazz standards and original compositions. It is Saturday night. The audience is energized. Is this a dream, evanescent, one that will disintegrate with daylight?

Behind me on the wall are large Chinese characters by the King of Kowloon. Do you know our graffiti scribbler, our street art man who has for years imprinted his curious non-language all over the walls and pillars of the city? Back in time, he might have been removed to the asylum at Castle Peak, the one which worried my youth with its knowable proximity. But we have become a more tolerant citizenry, with a wider vision and an eye for art. The writer and critic Lau Kin-wai brought this artist to his rightful place, through public exhibitions, and his strangely beautiful word-images form a permanent installation on the walls of this club, Blue Door. Lau is the founder of this art and performance space, one for diehard jazz aficionados like myself, because he too has a passion for the music and art and life as it can be in this city, and created this doorway to the larger world beyond our shores.

Kin-wai and I first met in 1996 at Tacheles, an arts center in the former East Berlin, the result of a Hong Kong–Berlin arts festival. He was one of the organizers of this artistic exchange, and I was one of two participating writers from Hong Kong. He spoke of Prague, to where he was headed, and of art and books and music and dance, and asked if I would join the group going there. Regrettably, I could not. My public life as a writer was still in its infancy; the only reason I could attend the festival was by timing it with a business trip for my then job at *The Asian Wall Street Journal.* So I slipped into Berlin for a few days to indulge the Muse, and slipped out to Amsterdam where the demands of newspaper distribution summoned my attention.

It was a pleasure to re-encounter Kin-wai regularly at Visage, the hairdresser's overlooking Lyndhurt Terrace that morphed into a bar on Saturday nights. That Visage no longer exists, vanished like so many faces of the city. Local jazz, rock and blues players showed up to jam. Poets, journalists, photographers, artists were the people you encountered. On one level, an alternative booze joint; on another, the respite at the top of a stairway climb where we spoke some of the same language some of the same time, when "post '97" could just be the name of a trendy club and not the era of our lives.

Kin-wai and I often talked at Visage till late, because both our homes were within easy walking distance. It was a transformative time for the city as we wondered aloud if this world we inhabited could last. He was hopeful: if there is still art, and jazz, and dance, and people with whom to share wine and words, and this place for awhile, has not life given us enough? I tiptoed around hope, conflicted as I was then between corporate life and the invitation of my Muse to surrender to the writer's life completely. Is the siren's song inevitable in life's journey? Odysseus stopped his crew's ears with wax, even as he, lashed to the mast, listened, indulged.

Mr. Visage himself often sat in the doorway, welcoming "club members," a universal euphemism for customers in bars without a liquor license. His ponytail fell long down his skinny back. If it got late enough and the crowd was not too rowdy, he would talk about the ghost stories he wanted to write. It was invariably the same, sober conversation. Ten ghost stories, ten lost lives. Such familiarity was soothing on a Saturday night at the end of another Hong Kong work week, seventy-plus hours of too much travel and too many phone calls, conversations, emails, and the terminal trance of spreadsheets, forcing meaning into numbers instead of words.

Doorways to the life of desire are often dark, clouded by smoke, enhanced by drink, relegated by daylight to hangover remedies and deep tinted shades. In the eighties, I learned to love dark entryways into the jazz clubs of American cities and towns — Cincinnati, Chicago, Philadelphia, Baltimore, DC, Brattleboro, Amherst, Springfield, Hartford, Aspen, Denver, L.A. *el al,* and of course, New York — everywhere my guitarist ex-husband sat in or gigged. The early nineties brought us back to Asia. It was the best and worst of times for jazz in Hong Kong. The Jazz Club had come into existence, and you could sometimes hear Eugene Pao or Ted Lo there, backing up a visiting international player or performing with a local band. Tony Carpio and his big band held court on Sunday afternoons at the Dickens Bar in the basement of the Excelsior. There were gigs and even people who listened. Things, as they say, could have been worse.

Yet when Joanne Brackeen arrived from New York to perform, she looked around at the fancy mall where a piano sat on a lonely podium. Live background music, presented as a cut above muzak, to delight passers-by for a moment in between their serious business of shopping. Was I ashamed of my city's crass commercialism that prevailed, that could not differentiate between real and fake music, that did not have a clue about booking a "jazz performance"? Yes, yes, and yes, because I could not thrice deny my connection to this place. Ms Brackeen did not flinch, and like a true artist, rose to the performance despite the impoverished surroundings. For an hour or so, her sparkling solos drowned the siren song of commerce, and perhaps for a moment, penetrated the wax of a handful of listening souls.

Jazz, that improvisatory music of dances, dirges, defiance and dissonance, was the America I carried home in the nineties. She proved a punitive muse, a constant reminder of my own artistic underlife in whose doorways I lurked while filling the family bowl from the rice cooker of commerce. The local economy was almost but not quite peaking; the Asian economic crisis hovered till the day after the handover. It was an undeniably good time to be a business world drone, when companies were hiring each and every day, when localization meant that to be Asian was to be wanted, when annual salary increases were *de rigueur. Come home,* I told my sister, fatigued as she was by London life, *you'll find a job in no time.* She did and was well employed in ten days, just by answering want ads in the *South China Morning Post.* After my own leaner years in New York City, where bosses warned you to start looking before the layoffs hit, it was a pleasure and relief not to count pennies that now rained from the heavens.

Besides, so much else was happening. Filmmakers were filming, photographers clicking, while artists painted and installed and performers turned city streets and corners into havens for expression. Even the writers were writing, in Chinese of course but also in English, imagine! Before and after the workday, you could measure life in teacups and shot glasses, pick at its pleasures with slender chopsticks, even hear jazz more than fortnightly, which was the way it had been twenty years earlier, the only jazz in town played at the top of the Arts Center. What more should this wide-eyed local girl want?

There were times I thought, was I finally home to stay?

Doorways, though, are where we dawdle and linger, considering possibilities, trying to decide. In our indecision, Fortune frowns, impatient. Jazz clubs come and go, as do the gigs and musicians. Today, Ted Lo recalls Oscar Peterson or Bill Evans. Tomorrow, Jason Cheng invokes Lenny Tristano or Bud Powell or Art Tatum, continuing the traditions of piano jazz.

In 2001, a new Asian culture rag in New York City commissioned me to write about jazz in Hong Kong. The East Coast liberal intellectual first-time editor said she wanted the "real thing," an insider's view, an essay on the state of this global music in our bit of the globe, and not just a travel guide piece. She spoke of the opportunity for Serious Writing as opposed to pop journalism. I hesitated, unsure, because I was neither a music journalist nor true jazz expert, only someone who loved the music and knew what life was like for jazz musicians. Could I do my city's jazz scene justice? Passion does however fire the senses and I agreed.

New York jazz had gone a little quiet for awhile. There was always some music, as well as a few new clubs. But the city's long road to economic recovery from the energetic eighties was still a little ragged at the edges, and jazz was just another industry that saw its fortunes fall or rise. By contrast, Hong Kong had already moved beyond the Asian Economic Crisis, and jazz, albeit a fringe art form, seemed to have hung in there and crossed over to some popular appeal.

The local musicians were generous with their time for interviews. I had anticipated that, but did not quite expect the rush of feeling that flowed from some. On the one hand, many acknowledged that a working musician could survive in Hong Kong, playing back up for Canto-pop stars, scoring music for films and commercials, doing hotel and other pseudo-jazz gigs to support real jazz performances that still happened. There were more foreign jazz musicians than ever to replace or add to those who originally brought the music to these shores — Americans naturally, but also Filipinos, South Americans, Europeans, Africans, Canadians, British and Australian — and the contemporary scene was evidence of that. By 2001, a significant number of good local musicians had appeared on the scene; some had returned from abroad, others had grown in stature as performers, the younger ones took advantage of the foreign musicians around to take lessons. But the musicians also told me that it was hard to get Hong Kong to care about the real thing, or even music standards for that matter. They pointed to racist attitudes towards Filipinos or African Americans that influenced perception. The lack of music education in local schools did not help matters. As one musician said, what she couldn't understand was why so many aspiring Canto-pop singers didn't even bother to learn how to sing properly, considering they wanted to perform. Hong Kong, they said, only cared about the surface of things, and that was true in music, which affected everything to do with jazz.

Yet it was also clear that almost all the musicians I interviewed were not simply complaining. Of course playing jazz was hard, but if you cared enough you would keep at it. Asian musical influences crept into compositions and performances, creating exciting fusions. Also, Hong Kong offered the opportunity to jam with great jazz players passing through from all over the world. Despite everything, there was a space for jazz. You could help create it. So I took my notes, wrote as balanced and comprehensive a piece as the word count allowed, and turned it into the magazine.

The surprise was the editor's final response: her board of directors insisted she kill the piece, which she did. The jazz scene in Hong Kong was nothing like that, I was told. The directors knew American musicians who had played in the hotels who said there were lots of gigs and that local audiences loved jazz. Of course, the musicians they referred to were visitors to the city, part of the five-star international hotel circuit gig scene, the "jazz gigs" that most local musicians do not get hired for. Well, I thought, so much for the "real insider thing."

Since then, Jazz at Lincoln Center has opened its doors in New York and, despite a huge fanfare at its launch, is still unable to fill the room completely with the real thing. It has also become fashionable for fading pop stars to record jazz standards (usually badly) to keep their careers going, because the music is seeing a revival among those too young to know or even care about the real thing. We open doors to one reality only to find another lurking behind it, waiting to be the next real deal. Somewhere, "the music box plays on," preserving, repeating, enhancing traditions. Jazz persists in Hong Kong because some play it and some listen, and for a little while, these isles are alive with sounds that remind us: we still belong to a world of multiple choices, multiple identities, multiple passions.

Last night, I lurked in the doorway of Gecko, the club in a SOHO alleyway next to the gay scene at Propaganda. This is "South of Hollywood Road" SOHO of Hong Kong, not the ones of London or New York. It was Wednesday, a good night to lurk, because the weekly jazz jam was in play, led by Jason on piano. Ginger Kwan sang.

A memory: recalling the voice of Angelita Li, an amazing vocalist of mixed Malaysian, Indian, Filipino and Chinese ethnicity from Hong Kong who used to be a regular on the scene. Her dark complexion made life tough, she told me a few years earlier. "The girls at school called me '*hark gwai,*' meaning 'black devil.'" Born into a musical family, she left for Bangkok and Los Angeles to further a career where her voice mattered more than skin color. When she came home, she rapidly became a top jazz singer in town, attracting a following with her skillful repertoire of standards and Brazilian fusion. Fluent in four languages, she has recorded jazz in Mandarin. Now she sings in Singapore, Hong Kong's loss, that island city's gain. Both millenniums have come and gone — the way Angelita has from this city, albeit close enough to return occasionally — as has the global bug fiasco of Y2K. Did the geeks of the world really program the 20th century to last forever?

Inside Gecko, it was relatively quiet, unlike the sometimes jam-packed, *voulez-vous coucher avec moi* nights, the pick up scene for which the club is also known. Jason called "Darn That Dream," fast, an oxymoronic upbeat, up tempo rendition that could almost be a hymn to jazz in this city. He is a BBC, who affects a range of British and Chinese accents on cue. Bandleader, entertainer, ivory tickler. A serious jazz musician who rolls with the rhythm of the times, playing for the dancers, drinkers, philistines and purists alike, but playing, always playing, playing.

From the doorway, a view of the *pissoir* and piano. Paul Candelaria on bass next to Jason, guitarist Skip Moy half visible around the corner of the entrance corridor, DC on his drums hidden inside the club. This was no more or less a stage than Joanne's piano podium in the mall. It wasn't so long ago that I listened to Ted solo in an atrium, at an upscale mall restaurant serving oysters and other delicacies, or to Eugene high up on a stage at a large, noisy bar cum restaurant for the young Chinese in crowd, few of who paid attention to the music "up there," or to Allen Youngblood performing original music in an empty basement room while the drinkers crowded the bar above. Should we apologize for the paucity of our jazz spaces, even those that try but cannot fill a room? The current Visage, hidden in an alley at the western end of SOHO, held an audience of six for a two-hour, acoustic, two-guitar concert by Eugene and Ken Rose. It is always a concert, as long as musicians play their heart and someone listens.

The very first night I sat with Kin-wai at a Blue Door jazz performance, he gestured at the space. His hands seemed to say *this is here, this is now, take it and make it yours.* His son, also an ardent jazz fan, came home after college in Australia and now manages day-to-day operations. More than a decade has passed since Kin-wai and I first talked music and art. We both drink less, stay out late less, reflect and write more. Age has its advantages.

The room was two-thirds full but every table was listening. We could have been back in the Jazz Club, circa 1997, the last audience for the last set on a week night while a local band traded improvisations into an almost empty room. Kin-wai was in a good mood, and proud. The jazz musicians are willing to play here, he told me, by which he meant the serious performers who treat the music as the art form it is. He was happy to have done his small share in keeping some jazz alive. It was more or less what he had once said about the King of Kowloon and the art he helped preserve.

Somewhere in this city tonight, someone will tune into "Uncle Ray" and listen all the way into morning. I hope it is a young person, ignorant, the way I once was as a thirteen-year-old, listening for the first time to Erroll Garner's "Misty" on radio, knowing this was not the polite classical music I had been taught to play. "Uncle Ray" wasn't spinning jazz and nostalgia then, but Tony Orchez was, opening the door to a future I could not have begun to imagine.

The door of Gecko is etched with a spirally Asiatic design. If you stare long enough at the center, after a couple of glasses of red wine on a rainy spring night, a shape emerges of the profile of a one-eared rabbit. As every Chinese child knows, moonglow means a rabbit is visible on the lunar surface. As every jazz player knows, the changes to the tune "Moonglow" will harmonize, more or less, "Heart & Soul" and a number of other standards. We pay small tribute where we can, preserving the memories that cross our doorways. In 1934, Will Hudson, Eddie DeLange and Irving Mills wrote the tune and lyrics that end like this: *"And now when there's Moonglow / Way up in the blue, / I always remember / That Moonglow gave me you."*

Bunny One Ear, deformed, mutilated or perhaps just contrary, daring to be different. A trope to evoke the jazz of my city that I have been privileged to hear and love.

IMPERMANENT ABODE

On my "permanent identity card," my HKID, it says I have the "right of abode in Hong Kong." There is an obsolete meaning for "abode" by the way, defined as a "temporary stay." I ponder this as I head towards the Department of Immigration for my appointment. The time has come to exchange my old card for a new "smart card," one that is computerized, durable, future-ready.

For years, my favorite uncle on my father's side has argued with me about what he considers my impermanent abode status. "Why the bloody hell don't you find a way to get the three stars on your card?" he demands in English with Sino-Bahasa characteristics, our usual medium of conversation. "I did." He is still an Indonesian citizen who, like me, once changed our Chinese surnames to Indonesian ones, the way many *wah kiu* did during Suharto's regime. Names, however, have little to do with true identity, and even less to do with what you know yourself to be. My uncle has always known that our family can claim a Chinese heritage, despite Indonesian and Hong Kong government bureaucracies. We were all given Chinese names at birth. Those of us who live in Hong Kong function in Chinese. Until we scattered from our Central Java *heung ha,* the family even maintained generational naming patterns. In Hong Kong, however, unless you have a Chinese name on your birth certificate, or can prove ethnicity through generational bloodlines, even those entitled to a permanent right of abode will not be granted the three stars for identity.

So there I was, headed down into the basement of Tsimshatsui Centre to get smart, toting memory-baggage of stars and other bureaucracies.

Eleven years earlier, in '96, I had trekked to Immigration Tower in Wanchai on a similar mission. Having carelessly lost my wallet, I needed a replacement card. At that time, it had been some years since I'd had to deal with any government department. Even though I was working and living in Asia, and had been since '92, full-time employment with major multinationals eased the processing of all necessary documentation and Inland Revenue collected my taxes with frightening efficiency. So I was slightly taken aback when the photo taker glanced at the paperwork, stared at me and demanded in Cantonese, "Aren't you Chinese? Why don't you have three stars?" Was this "civil" service, to be assailed by hostility when I was already frustrated by the loss of my card?

"Why?" I asked him. "Do I need them?"

"Don't you want a *wui heung jing?*" he countered.

I hesitated over this reference to, literally, the "return to your village" or "homecoming" identity document that facilitates border crossings into the Mainland for Hong Kong citizens. Only the three-star mark on your HKID allows this. My previous trips had meant expensive visas in my U.S. passport. This appeal to my instinctive pragmatism over a money-saving scheme created an immediate cultural impasse.

"It's easy," he continued, sensing an advantage. "As long as you were born here you can just tell them to include it."

The woman working alongside him chimed in. "Yes, you should do it now before the card is made. Just go back to the window and they'll take care of it."

For the first time in my life, I seriously considered the possibility. Perhaps it was the proximity of the handover, or the uncertain state of having lost my identity (albeit just a card, although my passport had disappeared with my wallet as well, rendering me entirely without any current proof of who I said I was), or the conviction of these two minor government officials that yes, we all should be "Chinese," whatever that meant. I vacillated a moment longer before saying, "No, it's okay. I don't need them."

The three stars are a throwback to a peculiar racial divide of colonial Hong Kong that is still extant. Race was the primary determinant of who was or wasn't considered "qualified" for a permanent right of abode; the other factor was birthplace. Until the handover, this wasn't a particularly hot issue in anyone's mind since the overwhelming majority of Hong Kong citizens were, and are, ethnically Chinese.

But passport immigration, globalization, interracial marriages and the human rights of ethnic minorities in any civilized society affect contemporary Hong Kong in this regard. The status of thousands of non-Chinese (especially South Asian) permanent residents, many of whose families have called this city home for generations and who contribute significantly to the economy and culture, emerged as a troubling social issue at the handover. The fate of the children of Mainland Chinese immigrants is a related problem: although ethnicity is not in question, the parents' place of birth and circumstance of entry can complicate matters. Who has the right to be both Hong Kong and Chinese in terms of identity and abode?

The so-called "facts" of this strange three-star fiction are ultimately unimportant, if you judge by the speculative blogging and queries online on the subject. If you search the government's official website, little of substance is available. From personal experience, I know of several individuals who fell through bureaucratic cracks and got the three stars, despite a nebulous ethnic history. When I inquired at Immigration over the years about my own situation, I invariably received different answers each time as to my eligibility, i.e.: yes, no, maybe, and my favorite, "try." The truth is that Hong Kong would prefer not to rule too clearly on this issue as long as the fussing few do not make international headlines.

So there I was, headed down the hallway towards the Smart Card application center, wondering yet again about the nature of permanent abodes.

You cannot really complain about government inefficiency in this city. Offices function, forms download, telephone hotlines do provide information. The transfer to the hyper-new, space-age Smart Identity Card was a triumph of public relations diplomacy, at least at the Tsimshatsui Centre. The mostly young officers peopling the desk were bright, polite and very, very well briefed to answer questions by the muddle-headed, middle-aged group into which I fell. By organizing the transfer exercise based on year of birth, the government ensured that similar FAQ's and confusions would be generationally sorted. There we were, in our age-defying state, dressed either too young or too old but rarely just right, waiting to be called by "Atheena" or "Hitem" or "Andi" or "Meiry" — their name plates proudly displaying globalized English-Chinese nomenclature — those sweet young Hong Kong women and men, all of who undoubtedly had three-star permanent identities.

This time, no one even whispered three stars. The sweet young things looked at my foreign legal name and spoke English first until I responded in Cantonese. The convenience of three-star, cross-border facilitation was no longer a consideration even though post 9-11, visa fees to China for U.S. citizens have risen sharply in retaliation to the U.S. raising the bar on entry for Chinese nationals. This was post-handover, 21st century Hong Kong, where race, apparently, matters less and less.

Yet now, when I slide my HKID with its golden chip into the card reader at the airport or train station, allowing me to zip rapidly through Immigration once my thumb print is confirmed, I feel less certain of the permanent nature of my promised abode.

What does it mean to be Chinese? I have often envied American friends who don't seem to question their American-ness the way we ethnic Chinese ponder our Chinese-ness. Hong Kong, in particular, both evades and confronts this question, sometimes dismissing it, and at others, insisting on its deep and profound importance. My extended *wah kiu* family, with its mixed Asian blood, has produced some members who look more Chinese than others. I am one of the indeterminates, the Asian being whom strangers address in every tongue from Korean to Tagalog to Putonghua to Bahasa to Japanese and also, Cantonese or English.

How racist are we really? The Great Wall was originally erected to prevent invasion by the "barbarians." It does, however, demarcate the world of the Han, even though Uygars and other minorities live within those walls. Hong Kong is unwalled, and it is unlikely anyone would consider the need for a wall to bring us into China.

But the lack of a physical boundary does not denote the absence of a mental one. For all our international sense of self, those three stars linger as an odd manifestation of what is a race-based outlook. A recent Letter to the Editor of the *South China Morning Post* questioned Chinese-ness in terms of language. Why, demanded the writer, do Hong Kong people not learn to speak Chinese properly? He went on to say that students were laughed at for bad English, but not for bad Putonghua, noting that Hong Kong parents maintain a mistaken belief that the language was easy to learn and thus considered its study and mastery unimportant. One man's opinion only, but he was not wrong in pointing out that the elite schools are all English medium, where English takes precedence over Putonghua. The flip side to that argument, which we hear frequently, is that the local English standard is in sad decline. Language is a long-standing conundrum here, as educators know only too well.

Perhaps the reason this language debate continues — now with the added question of China's official language — is that Hong Kong really cannot make up its mind just how Chinese it wants to be. We vacillate and sway, using terms like "permanent" to reassure us that no matter what, this tiny territory will abide as an abode, if we say it is so. Life is impermanent anyway, our pragmatic souls whisper, and in response we say "shhh, don't tell Beijing" and carry on living the way we do, imprinting stars on our cards to bolster our will to survive.

The last time my uncle and I knocked back a few beers together, he mentioned the three stars again. He is my favorite uncle for many reasons, not the least of which is the close relationship he had with my late father, his cousin. We may laugh at my uncle's atonal Cantonese — despite his wife who is fluent in Cantonese and Mandarin my uncle never mastered Chinese completely — but without him, I would not have learned to play poker or blackjack or to ride a bicycle. "It's a marvelous city," he says of Hong Kong, echoing my father, as we watch sunset over the harbor. Perhaps the three stars he managed to acquire offer something more important than permanence. Perhaps they assure him that regardless of where he came from, this is where he knows he wants to be.

coda

. . . so that we will not simply gloss over endings

A SHORT HISTORY OF OUR SHORES
as told to the author by the City of Hong Kong

Note by author: *The City speaks of itself in first person plural, in what native English speakers think of as the "royal we." A more accurate interpretation is the collective Chinese we, a plural that embraces the clan or society to which an individual belongs. Hong Kong, after all, does not think in English, even though it can, and in our interview, it chose to speak in "Canto-lish," mostly Cantonese with a dash of English. The English language concept of "singular" and "plural" does not have an exact equivalent in Chinese grammar.*

C all us Hong Kong. That *was* our name. Our new one is "Xianggang" because in China, Putonghua (or Mandarin) is the lingo, not Cantonese or English, and *pinyin* with all its x's and double g's is the transliteration of choice. Of course, "Hong Kong" is neither Cantonese (*Heung Gong)* nor English (Fragrant Harbour), but it *was* the name that stuck. Today, our acronym is the S.A.R. ("Special Administrative Region" being such a mouthful), but for a brief while there, it was an embarrassing moniker because to the whole world, we were "S.A.R.S. City," a plague on humankind.

But the world still calls us Hong Kong.

For all you folks who stop by, or even stay awhile, we still have that buzz, that excitement, that electric, nervy energy. Ask an American or a British or a Japanese or even a Chinese who's been our way before — *has the city changed much since the "handover" to China* — and you will likely be told, *no, it's still a capitalist paradise.*

That's the problem when you do the slow dissolve. It tricks the eye and all the other senses as well. What folks don't see is our quiet disappearance. We've got our pride. We don't want to exit kicking and screaming, dragged away in chains by the People's Liberation Army (PLA). Besides, the PLA has better things to do with its time. The problem is, it's not like we wanted to fade out; we just don't have much choice, not really.

Oh, it's not as if no one pays attention. The symptoms of our malady are recorded, even if the diagnosis is neither useful nor objective. CNN, the BBC and other first world media laud all our democracy marches, pretty much the way they praised Tiananmen protesters back in '89. Meanwhile, over on the Mainland (the "Big Six" in our Cantonese homonym for the People's Republic), hundreds of thousands of Chinese citizens still don't know Tiananmen ever happened. You can bet your bottom *renmenbi* Beijing doesn't know or care that our citizens are unhappy with the way things are or the way things are becoming.

The trouble with politics is, well, it's so *political.* Look at us: Asia's fashion capital; the Oriental pearl; the land of Jackie Chan, spinning through celluloid heaven; the ultimate trading haven where the rich get richer and the Jockey Club funds the services for the poor. We out-gamble Macau any day and the revenue is sizeable enough to make a significant dent in social welfare. Communism? That hot, kitschy trend of Mao caps and Red Books flying out of factories at the speed of "genuine" antiques? If you make it, they will come and if you sell it, they will buy. Us vote? We'd rather go shopping.

But we didn't expect this vanishing.

Who will remember us when we're just another Chinese city? Will our legacy be Jackie's films? Wong Kar Wai's? Or an "American Idol" like William Hung who "can't sing, can't dance" but is a super Hong Kong star? Will we become Orientalist nostalgia for the West, the way Shanghai still is, and will genuine "made in Hong Kong" junk go for thousands on E-Bay? What of our former colonial self? Will the last of our Canto-British civil servants live out retirement sipping "milk-tea" in London, giddily chanting "in Hong Kong, they strike a gong and fire the noonday gun?" The cannon still goes off, you know, even if the streets are cleared of Noel Coward's mad dogs and Englishmen. What of our Canto-pop stars? Have their fifteen minutes already passed now that Mando-rap's the rage? Or is our contribution to the world's heritage *dim sum,* the "little hearts" of tasty morsels that tease but do not satiate? And is the "Hong Kong identity" that local artists and intellectuals claimed before the handover still extant? Or will that too be gone with the gusts that visit our South China Seas?

Should we, like the Bard, be content to emote — *No longer mourn for us when we are dead?* If a sea-swimming mammal could immortalize Ishmael, cannot an entire island (and a Mainland peninsula and land mass, plus all those outlying islands) do likewise for us?

We are Hong Kong, a "city-village" of the world. We want to live in the global collective imagination. Allow us now to ruminate, reflect, despair, rejoice, celebrate, recall and *record* the space of history we were, the space in the world we are, and let us sing an ode to the city we may eventually become.

Here then, is a short history of our shores.

Some years ago — never mind how long precisely — having little or no resources to speak of, and nothing in particular to interest the world — we were home to a handful of aboriginal fisher folk. One myth says they were descendants of a sexual liaison between a princess and a hound. So there we were, an archipelago of 235 islands and rocks in the middle of the South China Sea, hunkering down whenever typhoons raged, home to the mongrel caste.

Mythmaking is however not our whole story. Six thousand years ago, as far back as the Neolithic Age, it's quite likely that some Chinese inhabited our shores. Excavated tombs, cliff carvings, artifacts from various historical periods point to a cultural connection with North and South China. The Baiyue tribe that peopled China's southeastern coast were probably the real native Hong Kongers. A little fish and salt didn't hurt their diet, and pearl fishing put our Tolo Harbor (formerly, Meichuan) on China's map of commerce during the Song Dynasty, sometime around 791 AD. But in the words and music of Mitch and Hoagy (we try to keep up with the rest of the world), *that was long ago and now my consolation is in the stardust of a song.*

Through much our history, the Motherland ignored us. Only Hainan Island, to the west and further south, was more ignominious, scorned as the "end of the earth" and which became an exile for errant politicos, or, in recent years, off-course U.S. military pilots. Of course *now*, Hainan's celebrated as "China's Hawaii" and is regularly visited by Beijing's top brass. Lazy Paradise! Miserable fraud! Flattered, nonetheless.

Enough with envy. Our elders caution against such needless energy waste. Back instead to our story.

In 1729, which was the era of the Qing, we got castigated in a provincial report because, it seems, the folks on our shores were a little too fond of gambling: "Gamblers are worse than mere idlers. They neglect their proper occupations and waste away their family fortunes . . . We consider the reason why gambling proliferates is that when fathers and elder brothers indulge in it, their sons and younger brothers take notice and emulate them; when masters indulge, their slaves and servants observe and copy them; and even women and young girls fall into the slough and do not think it blameworthy; and because so many are addicted many more become corrupted." The report added that magistrates who discovered and punished manufacturers of "gambling equipment" would be rewarded with promotion under a new scheme.

The problem with the ruling class is their fondness for morality, or rather, the espousing of same. Falling "into the slough" doesn't strike us as nearly so bad as binding and crippling the feet of young girls for male sexual longings and female sadistic tendencies. Still, ours was not to reason why, just to nod and tune out the mutterings from above. No one *really* listens to the ruling class, right? Beijing was far enough away and could be safely ignored, requiring at least a fortnight's journey on the back of a tiger (and we had tigers back then, as well as leopards, wild cats and boars, pangolins, thirty-two varieties of serpents and two hundred species of butterflies). The big cats are gone now — although you can savor the odd pangolin, illegally, up north in Guangzhou — but the serpents and butterflies still abound. Today the Jockey Club (formerly "Royal," now the club of the people with means) funds a host of vital social services that taxes alone cannot. So gamble, we must.

Until we stepped into that "foreign mud," the slough of opium, we mean. Don't blame us. There we were, minding our business as a territory with a hospitable harbor for pirates and traders. Did *we* sprout poppies (specifically, the *papaver somniferum)* from our soil? Inspissate the juice? Roll out those reddish-brown, malodorous and bitter-tasting cakes, balls and sticks of the soporific drug? Moreover, did we insist the British sail through our waters with ship loads of the junk from India? No. We were just a peace-loving transit point, with a few folks making the odd buck on that noisome trade, providing a den or two for addicts. Mind you, the *hordes* of addicts were on the Mainland, the "Celestial Kingdom" as China named herself. We made no such claims to grandeur, being only a "fragrant" or possibly "Incense Harbor," fragrant being a homonym for incense in Cantonese. We no longer insist on the latter name, since the former stuck, but confidentially, the fragrance was wistful English romanticism, the British being true sentimentalists rather than true adventurers at heart.

The war that resulted was all about "free trade." The British were selling, the Chinese were buying until it became undeniably evident that opium was bad for the health of the citizenry. In 1839, no surgeon general issued bland and polite warnings on packets of opium. So Chinese officials did the next best thing: they seized and destroyed shipments of the drug. Such assault on "free trade" did not amuse the British, anymore than did the soaking of tea in Boston's harbor more than sixty years prior. The trouble with the ruling class is that they lack a sense of humor and simply don't learn from history, which is why we think history might as well be short.

The Opium War made us who we are, the war and Charles Elliot.

A word on old Chas — such a historically unfortunate name because even on the internet he's merely one of many so christened — he's the chap who hit the diplomatic skids by acquiring a small, hilly, granite island in the Landrone chain for the British as victorious war spoils. Lord Palmerston was disgusted with the negotiations effected by this Superintendent of Trade who "disobeyed" orders to bargain hard and well. Palmerston expected much more than a "barren rock," while Prince Albert, the queen's husband, was "so much amused at my having got the island of Hong Kong," as Victoria quipped in a letter to her uncle, the King of Belgium. Dear Victoria was more amused than she usually let on.

Poor Chas just couldn't win. From China's perspective, the country was suffering a trade deficit, its silver being drained away while its citizens were zoning out their futures. What else could they do but seize and destroy the vile substance? Meanwhile, along came Chas, indignant, aggressive even, demanding seven million Mexican silver dollars for the loss of "goods." Do you wonder that he was told to take a hike? Gunboat diplomacy is, however, persuasive, which Chas exercised, but he might have been a wee bit overconfident when he claimed Hong Kong for Britain even before any treaty was signed. But on one point he wasn't wrong: our rocky island was the extraordinary vantage point he judged it to be — strategically and commercially — back then and to this day.

In the tradition of visionary expatriates of all nations, Elliot was scorned as an aggressor by China and dishonored and forgotten by Britain. He was posted initially to Texas as the *charge d'affaires,* where he failed in his quest to prevent the state's annexation to the U.S. This is what happened when he *obeyed* orders by his superiors, as he did in Texas, as opposed to follow his instincts, as he did on our shores. He later became governor of Bermuda, Trinidad and St. Helena, and died in Exeter at the age of seventy-four. His other claim to fame was having Port Elliot named for him in 1852, the coastal site of Australia's first railway (a disaster in its day due to huge cost overruns) where shipwrecks frequently occurred as ships attempted to navigate past difficult rocks off the coast. Port Elliot's economy later transformed to thrive on tourism and still does.

Poor Charles Elliot, we have named not even a *cul-de-sac* in his dis-honor.

So that's how we began, with an island shaped like half a plucked chicken and a town center named Victoria but more commonly thought of as Hong Kong. In a series of unequal treaties between Britain and China, Kowloon peninsula, with its sandy, phallic tip, and the New Territories rolled over into the empire, the latter "leased" for ninety-nine years beginning in 1898. Had the British placed greater trust in the ancient feudal system of slum lording, they would have known that in matters of real estate, it is always better to own than rent. The lease was in part their undoing because it had to run out, as China was quick to note round about 1984, and no one in their right mind by then would believe that *only* the New Territories would return to China. There's no longer any question that the treaties were unequal; perhaps an odd "iron-necked" colonial might dare say aloud that these were for the good of empire. He, and most assuredly it is a he, is either very old and dying or young and a re-inventor of history, a neo-con reactionary. At least we'd like to think so, wouldn't you?

Anyway, time marched on and we continued to be ignored — the philosophy, as such, being *laissez-faire* — and to a certain extent, we were "left to do" more or less what we wished. It wasn't exactly like being orphaned, more like residing at an English country boarding school without breaks for holidays or being confined to a study exile in Beijing to sit the Confucian-style civil service exams as many times as necessary until we passed (not unlike the American bar examinations). A prolonged adolescence remained our highest pinnacle of existence.

It was terribly post-modern of us, don't you think, to be so perpetually youthful? And the 20th century hadn't yet dawned, or modernism.

Our entry into the modern era was partly characterized by one man: Dr. Sun Yat-Sen.

A digression on youth. Even as late as the early seventies, the natives did not study much local history. Local civics, perhaps, and plenty of Chinese, English and even a bit of "world" history — Islam, various Franco-Prussian monarchs and republics, the Ottoman Empire, Woodrow Wilson, Hitler — but about our own history, the less said the better, or so it seemed. The mostly Southern Chinese natives who comprised 98% to 99% of the populace until very recent times were content with the Motherland's history as a substitute for their own, and the foreign natives clung to the histories of the nations whence they sprang. Thus, time marched on, unrecorded by a growing intellectual elite who preferred, initially, the dictates of Oxbridge, which enlarged to include the American Ivies and Canadian commonwealth where their historical canons did not see much point in "wasting saliva" on Hong Kong. We were, after all, only colonial, as opposed to post-colonial or self-liberated like our Northeast and Southeast Asian neighbors, all of who could claim the nation-state pride of flags, revolutions and history. We did however come up with a flag that no one can draw or remember.

Thus an absence of history in the collective consciousness, except for the venerable Dr. Sun.

In a primary school civics textbook, circa 1960, there is this Cantonese couplet: 孫中山先生╱我們登高山 "Sun Yat-Sen, Sir / We will climb the high hill." The text's authors were no doubt entranced by the rhyme of "Sir" and "hill" as a mnemonic for young charges to recall the name of the erstwhile gentleman, as there is no real reason for the juxtaposition. His name in Cantonese, by the way, is Suen Chung-san, derived from his Japanese name, Nakayama, adopted during his political exile. It is by this exile's Cantonese name that we best know him. We take for granted, naturally, that the whole world does indeed know of this founder of the first Chinese republic, but that, we have discovered, is not so, even among the relatively sophisticated and educated folks of the first world. So a word on the Hong Kong life of Dr. Sun, whose memory is commemorated on our shores along the shady streets the government today designates as historical landmarks, and whose presence on many shores — from Hawaii to Vancouver to France to Taiwan and numerous locations in the Motherland is widely recorded and revered, and who, unlike Charles Elliot, has the individual distinction of deserving "an annotated list of internet resources."

He first set foot in Hong Kong around 1883 after graduating from Honolulu's Oahu College at the age of seventeen. The problem with sending bright young boys to Anglican missionary schools in the west, which Hawaii more or less was despite its then independent state, is that they might find a god, which Sun most assuredly did. This was not the "journey to the west" his family had in mind. In an attempt to thwart his conversion to Christianity, his brother shipped him to our shores to "improve his English," which he did, ending up at Queen's College. Gods work in mysterious ways however and the young man converted to Christianity nonetheless.

Having improved his English, he returned to Canton (now, Guangzhou) to improve his Chinese studies. In this respect, Sun was a typical Chinese geek, studying hard to please his family while fomenting revolt in his spare time. In 1887, married two years to the first Madame Sun, he returned to our shores by transferring to the College of Medicine for Chinese. And here in the great tradition of overseas-Chinese, mostly-science students the world over, he did become a doctor while engaging in his version of 19th Century internet hacking, a.k.a. starting a revolution. We don't want to brag but we believe he liked our little city-village, and that we provided him some inspiration or example of what life could be like on the Motherland if only those corrupt and inefficient Beijing officials were ousted or at least, reformed. How he found time to shuttle between Hong Kong and Macau, as he frequently did, and attempt to organize a revolution to overthrow the Qings, and think through and write about the principles of revolution *and* still complete his medical studies with straight A's, we are sure we do not know. Passion has its own rewards, however, as his later years found him betrothed to and worshipped by a considerably younger woman (the final dream of all older, vital and even non-so-vital men), Ching-ling, the most glamorous Soong sister (aptly played in the film version by our illustrious actress Maggie Cheung).

Hawaii beckoned again, round about autumn of 1894, where he formed the Revive China Society, but by February of the following year, he returned to Hong Kong and established the society's headquarters here. In late October, Britain banned Sun from our shores when his second plot to capture Canton on October 26 failed. The "decree of banishment" was issued by one Stewart Lockhart on behalf of the local government and made quite clear that "this government has no intention of allowing the British colony of Hong Kong to be used as an Asylum for persons engaged in plots and dangerous conspiracies against a friendly neighbouring Empire." In the language of repression, the ruling classes invariably agree: former "enemies" can suddenly become "friends" when imperial rule is at stake.

The young revolutionary exiled himself in Japan, and then Hawaii, and found his way to Europe by fall of 1896. He remained barred from Hong Kong for several more years. We nurtured his youth and idealism, and have never completely lost our affection for him despite his ultimately ineffectual role in the course of history. The affection is mutual. In February, 1923, Dr. Sun addressed the students at the University of Hong Kong, saying he got his ideas for revolution and modernization "right here . . . Hong Kong impressed me a great deal because there was orderly calm and because there was artistic work being done without interruption."

Sun was our first true "astronaut" — a term coined for that phenomena of our natives who traverse the globe, most famously between Hong Kong and Vancouver for passport privileges in the eighties and early nineties — as he shuttled between China, Hong Kong, Japan, America, Britain, Europe, Taiwan in search of a base of operation, scattering and spreading his culture and sensibility wherever he touched down.

A brief coda on his fate. On January 1, 1912, the Revolutionary League set up the first Chinese Republic at Nanjing, with Sun as the provisional president. He surrendered that post three months later, inauspiciously if willingly, on April Fool's day to Yuan, the first president. Sun's dream of a revolution founded on his "Three People's Principles" — nationalism, democracy and socialism — was not to be. Nationalism prevailed at the expense of the other two. He died in 1925 at the age of 57 and did not live to see the 1931 invasion of his country by Japan, the same country that once provided a haven for his revolutionary activities. We wonder what he would have said to Mao and all the others that followed.

Should we climb his high hill, still?

Meanwhile, back to us. Our history and culture does get so muddled with that of the Motherland, inseparable as we are. The "orderly calm" that Sun admired was a view through somewhat rose-tinted lenses, and what "artistic work" he referred to might just as easily have been accomplished through the turmoil, corruption and disorder that also characterized our state. His predilection for revolt, it appears, left some imprint as we'll see in later years.

Racial and cultural segregation of Chinese and Westerners was the norm, which is another way of saying that the two groups couldn't stand the sight of each other. Years before Sun, the natives were already restless and inclined to overthrow their British, rather than their Chinese overlords. In 1857 a baker, one Cheong Ah Lum, in a fit of patriotic fervor, laced the loaves served to the English with arsenic. Some four hundred Europeans got severe indigestion as a result and Cheong was prosecuted but acquitted for murder due to a lack of evidence. The British rule of law prevailed admirably in this instance, as the jury comprised seven of his European victims. He was deported to China in the end, which just goes to show that if you don't like the prevailing conditions of life, attempting mass indigestion might get you a free ticket home.

But eschewing the restless natives does not a good colony make, and effective communication was more persuasive than the separation of state and bread (the bakery concession went to one George Duddell after the "affair of the poisoned bread," the same mogul who held the opium monopoly, proof positive that in "picking your poison" correctly, you will be further rewarded; *NB:* Duddell, unlike Elliot, does have an alley in Central named after him). The teaching of English created a Chinese elite whom the British could count on to be compradors, civil servants and professionals and who, being well fed, would not be too restless. By 1896, the Central School examination papers for Chinese students in local English schools required essays on topics such as the "special value to England of both Malta and Hong Kong" and "Benefits of Foreign Trade." We like to think that at least one young man might have, in answer to the latter, penned something to the effect of "The greatest benefit of foreign trade, as far as I can see, is to poison your enemies so that a new order might prevail, in some cases resulting in the unfettered expansion of an empire's territory," but we doubt he would have been accorded a passing grade.

So modernity dawned with a cosmopolitan, bi-literate, bi-cultural, local society, but one that still remained extremely Chinese. Perhaps more Chinese studied English than the reverse, but that is the way things were and still are. What some of the English studied and observed was the horror of local ways. Mrs. Haselwood was a case in point. Wife of the retired Lieutenant appointed Superintendent of the Naval Chart Depot, she arrived in the summer of 1919 and soon discovered the wholly un-Christian custom of "*mui tsai's*," the sale of young girls into indentured slavery for domestic or commercial purposes. In her 1930 book, *Child Slavery in Hong Kong,* she pointed out that these girls "are paid no wages for their work, and at the death or the whim of their employer they are liable to be resold to the first comer willing to purchase them. This possibility being always present in their mind, who will contend that their lot is anything but a cruel one, the cruelty being usually of so subtle a nature as not to be easy to prove or discover? Had the British Government from the very outset even prohibited *resale,* some of the worst horrors these girls have undergone in Hong Kong might have been averted, but no steps had been taken in this direction at any time by those responsible for the government of the colony."

Was this horror worse on our shores than back in Dickensian England of chimney sweeps and scullery maids? Or was this Chinese custom particularly egregious to her because we were a colony, a point of pride for the British Empire, where such inhumanity should not be tolerated? We cannot be sure now except to say that Mrs. Haselwood visited her moral judgment on this universal injustice and called upon both the perpetrators and the empowered to cease a practice which today continues in one form or another in the global "free trade" of human beings, so long as there are sellers and buyers.

By contrast, the Chinese writer Ba Jin (pen name for Li Feigan) found a strange moment of peace in Hong Kong from the revolution he fomented through literature and other subversions. Chinese artists and intellectuals often passed through our city-village between their forays to the West and the Motherland, but their concerns remained centered on the problems in China. There was always so much historical and cultural evolution happening across the border — May 4th, the new republics, political grandstanding and intrigue, the emergence of the likes of Mao Dun and Lu Xun in a burst of literary flowering, and all that oppressed peasantry just waiting to be liberated — that we were designated a pipsqueak of no consequence. Politically, we were an inconvenient pimple on China's cheek, waiting for the release of adolescent hormonal pus. The British and the odd Eurasian partied on the Peak while the Chinese found respite to express their cosmopolitan personae on our shores among faces like their own.

Like Ba Jin, born into a bureaucrat-landlord family, who reviled the old feudal system that to a certain extent characterized Hong Kong's *nouveau riche* culture of commerce. "The honesty of the working people and their bitter lot stirred up thoughts of rebellion in me," he wrote when a young man. "I said I didn't want to be a young master. I wanted to be on their side and help them." One of his stories, "A Moonlit Night" details the murder of a peasant who struggles against the tyrannical gentry. Ba Jin viewed us briefly in 1933, sailing past our shores by night and wrote that "the night was still and soft. Not a sound was to be heard from the shore; Hong Kong seemed to have shut its great mouth. Yet when I gazed upon the scintillating mountain of stars, I could hear the lights whispering to each other . . . Sight and hearing became confused, and I seemed to be listening with my eyes. The mountain of stars was hardly silent; it was performing a great symphony. I almost forgot where I was." Although charmed, he was not entirely fooled by the dream-like moment. There was more to us than met the eye, and even in his brief essay, he understood something of the tumult and confusion, enough to know that "it was another world there, full of noise and excitement. The moment I stepped into the cabin, I asked myself: 'Was everything I just saw an illusion?'"

1933 was notable, because the Japanese seized Manchuria that year and installed Pu Yi, the "last emperor," on the throne of that puppet kingdom Manchukuo, which was not entirely unlike our colonial state, except that we did not have so obvious and singular a puppet as Pu Yi. A chorus of Jiminy Crickets was more our speed, in the spirit of a Disney retelling of the richer, original *Pinnochio* by the Italian author Carlo Collodi. Puppetry is an ancient and venerable art form, and we should not be too quick to denigrate its value or historical significance.

Just as we were getting a little restless with our pimply state, the "world," or at least Europe erupted into a war that eclipsed the activity around us. When we think of WWII, however, Germany pales against Japan's military expansion in our region. On the morning of December 8, 1941 local time, the Japanese invaded our little city-village, only several hours after the attack on Pearl Harbor. Thirty-six Japanese light bombers rained from our skies that morning. On December 18, a hundred motorboats and dinghies with troops landed on our island's north shore. A week later, on "Black Christmas" day, the British surrendered us to Japan and our occupation formally began.

If you think we suffer from an "identity crisis" today, imagine how folks felt back then. As if learning English wasn't hard enough, were we now expected to speak Japanese as well, or be shot like an elderly woman on Queen's Road because she did not understand the lingo of the sentry who stopped her? "The war in Hong Kong," stated the occupation notices posted round the city, "is directed against the white men," which was meant to reassure all Chinese that they were safe. The trouble with the ruling class is that they are prone to lies, in which case a puppet with an elongated nose would at least be a useful indicator of what *not* to listen to.

Three years and eight months of stunted growth, such was the length of that occupation. Now we ask you, wouldn't you be ripe for revolt? Two young men, a worker Cai Guoling and an intellectual Chen Daming transformed their restlessness into action as leaders of the Hong Kong–Kowloon Independent Brigade, our resistance fighters against the Japanese.

At this point in our interview, the city heaved an enormous sigh of fatigue. It waved a dismissive isle at the writer, indicating our session was over. When pressed for a closing quote, the city began, "Our history is . . .," but was halted temporarily by a coughing fit.

"We are prone to respiratory ailments these days, and our eyes smart from the lack of sun and too many particulates," the city continued. "Sometimes, it's better to forget the way we were, to become extinct. We are a willfully forgetful citizenry, because to forget is to prosper and to prosper is to pave the way for dreams."

The city began to transform. Its shoreline receded or expanded, changed, reshaped itself into the hard angles of development. As the years ticked by, the masses were housed, buildings were demolished, the people prospered. The city twisted itself into a knot as the skies darkened and rainstorms deluged the streets with increasing frequency. The people became astronauts and flew to the moon — or somewhere just as desolate — and back. Money was lost, money was made. Years of real or manufactured significance were noted by visionaries and artists and just as quickly forgotten. 1967. 1979. 1984. 1987. 1997. The city hiccupped at that moment, shuddered and shriveled. "2012," it said. "We place small hope on 2012 before we concern ourselves with 2046. The historians can make what hay they wish while the sun still occasionally shines."

The city contracted S.A.R.S. but was cured. Its constitution was noticeably weakened, however.

"But what about our cosmopolitan identity?" I demanded, afraid the city would vanish before I could record all it had to say. "We can't just dismiss our colorful history, our unusual political state, our global positioning eye on the world. Can't we be Chinese like say, Shanghai?"

"Have you been to Shanghai lately? Not a bicycle in sight and a tangle of traffic even worse than Bangkok! We will not compare ourselves to that city of a thousand compromises!" The city sputtered noisily. "At least we have the I.C.A.C. At least we govern without corruption most of the time now, and we understand transparency some of the time."

"Then are we not equally as compromised?"

The city paused, ruminated, and then began to fade. As it assumed a vaporous, indistinct form, it finally said. "No, not compromised. Occupied. Perpetually occupied. Our history," and here the city smiled condescendingly. "Our history, my dear, is fiction."

I began to weep. What had begun as a promising and energetic declaration of our history had dissolved into less than nothingness. The trope that was my city had disintegrated into a literary joke. What was there left for a writer from our shores?

"Don't cry," said the city, kinder now. "Think of me as your silver city, spiraling through time. You know, like a gigantic *ngahn si gyun.*"

At the mention of the northern steamed bread, my sobs abated. Literally, the name means "silver slivers spiral." A soft, delicate mini baguette that is completely white and smooth outside, filled with soft white shreds, served warm as a side dish, horizontally sliced into three or four sections. "My sister loved those," I said. My tense construction did not escape either our notice.

"Of course I know," the city replied.

"She used to take the cone, scoop out the shreds, and fill the smooth hollowed out crust with steamed shrimps."

"I remember."

"It was a long time ago," I said, wiping my eyes. "Past, over, *waan yuen.*"

The city paused in its fadeout. "The game's not over till I say so. Watch me," it said.

And there before me flooded an image of the harbor skyline, panning west to where the view has undergone the greatest transformation. Two companion towers, IFC One and Two rose out of the earth — cold, phallic, curving upwards into an uncircumcised foreskin — in all their silvery pallor. I found myself on board the Star Ferry on a misty late winter morning, circa 2006, and the buildings *en masse* appeared to float above the mist. I was reminded of the paintings of Henry Brokman, a little-known Danish artist of the late 19th century who ended up in Sorrento. He painted the Italian coastline in a curiously silver light and mist which make his landscapes appear half-real; you could see his world, but the light was rendered to tease you, whispering, *catch me if you think you can.* The musical soundtrack's glittery voiceover: *See me. Feel me. Touch me. Heal me.*

"It's pollution, you know," whispered the city, as it began fading again. "Not nature."

"So will you return?"

"Maybe."

"Any last words?"

"My memory is your memory? The you being plural, naturally."

Then, the city vanished before my eyes. I watched, helpless.

What, indeed, was left?

Except to write. To insist, in language wild and even wicked, that we existed, we exist, we will exist, the way the Quixotes of our city continue to tilt at their paper windmills, regardless of the odds. Only then have we not been, will we not be, ignored, either by our colonial or Chinese overlords. Only then will the substance of our existence matter.

In a quarry far north in the state of Vermont, American poet Jody Gladding paints words onto both sides of small shards and slabs, gathered from that vast and empty space. She imagines life into the stones with the words she paints, words that can be read backwards and forward, because the top is the bottom and the front is the also the back. Words that loop like a neverending story into eternity. As pieces of my city disappear — a historic building here, a one-time landmark there, a dream of universal suffrage once promised by an occupier who could wash its hands clean of consequence — I find solace in the power of absence. This thought then from Gladding's *Quarry Project*, quoted from a work about installation artist Ann Hamilton, which speaks to the future of our city:

> the substance has tilted
> forward into
> consequence:
>
> from "it is matter"
> to "it matters":

We write because to write is to think is to imagine, regardless.

bibliography & references

The following PUBLICATIONS were consulted in the writing of this collection:

Abbas, Ackbar *Hong Kong: Culture and the Politics of Disappearance,* Hong Kong University Press, 1998.

Chan, Ming K. and Clark, David J. (editors) *The Hong Kong Basic Law: Blueprint for "Stability and Prosperity" under Chinese Sovereignty?* Hong Kong University Press, 1991.

Cheung, Martha P.Y. (editor) *Hong Kong Collage: Contemporary Stories and Writing,* Oxford University Press, Hong Kong/Oxford/New York, 1998.

Clarke, David *Hong Kong x 24 x 365: A Year in the Life of a City,* Hong Kong University Press, 2007.

Coetzee, J.M. "As a Woman Grows Older," *The New York Review of Books,* January 15, 2004, pp. 11–14.

Coetzee, J.M. *Elizabeth Costello,* Viking, New York, 2003.

Dong, Stella *Sun Yat-sen: The Man Who Changed China,* FormAsia, Hong Kong, 2004.

Fairbank, John King *China: A New History,* The Belknap Press of Harvard University Press, Cambridge/London, 1992.

Fok, K.C. *Lectures on Hong Kong History: Hong Kong's Role in Modern Chinese History,* The Commercial Press (Hong Kong) Ltd., 1990.

Hsu, Immanuel C.Y. *The Rise of Modern China,* Oxford University Press, Hong Kong/Delhi/Melbourne/Kuala Lumpur, 1979.

Lam, Agnes *Water Wood Pure Splendour,* Asia 2000 Ltd., Hong Kong, 2001.

Leung, Ping-kwan *City at the End of Time* (translated by Gordon T. Osing), Twilight Books Company in association with Department of Comparative Literature University of Hong Kong Cultural Studies Series Nr 3, 1992.

Liu, Shuyong *An Outline History of Hong Kong,* Foreign Language Press, Beijing, 1997.

Morris, Jan *Hong Kong: The Final Edition,* Penguin Books, 1997.

Said, Edward W. *Culture and Imperialism,* Vintage Books, New York, 1994.

Said, Edward W. *Orientalism,* Vintage Books, New York, 1979.

Simon, Joan *Ann Hamilton,* Harry Abrams, NY, 2002, p. 195.

Spence, Jonathan *The Search for Modern China,* Century Hutchinson Ltd., London, 1990.

Thiong'o, Ngugi wa *Decolonising the Mind,* James Curry Ltd., Oxford & EAEP, Nairobi & Heinemann, Portsmouth, New Hampshire, 2003.

This Is the Ultimate Fake Book, 3rd ed. (C instruments), Hal Leonard Corp., Milwaukee, Wisconsin.

Tsang, Steve *A Modern History of Hong Kong,* Hong Kong University Press, 2004.

Waley, Arthur (translator) *The Book of Songs,* Grove Press, Inc., New York, 1978.

White, Barbara-Sue (editor) *Hong Kong: Somewhere between Heaven and Earth, An Anthology,* Oxford University Press, Hong Kong/Oxford/New York, 1996.

The following ONLINE RESOURCES were used:

Asia Times
China Daily
Google
Government of the Hong Kong Special Administrative Region of the People's Republic of China, The http://www.gov.hk/
http://www.theguitarguy.com/houseofb.htm
IMDb http://www.imdb.com/
International Lyrics Playground http://lyricsplayground.com/
Lyrics Freak http://www.lyricsfreak.com/
Merriam Webster *The Unabridged Dictionary*
MP3 Lyrics Organized http://www.mp3lyrics.org/
New York Times, The
South China Morning Post
Wikipedia
http://williamhung.net

DICTIONARIES referenced for romanization & translation:

Note on romanization: For all Putonghua (Mandarin) references, standard pinyin has been used unless otherwise specified. Cantonese follows Yale Romanization except for some generally accepted alternatives commonly used in Hong Kong (e.g.: *dimsum)*

Cantonese *Chinese-English Dictionary* (Cantonese in Yale Romanization/ Mandarin in Pinyin), ed. Chik Hon Man and Ng Lam Sim Yuk, New Asia Yale-in-China Chinese Language Centre, The Chinese University of Hong Kong, 1994.

English *English-Cantonese Dictionary* (Cantonese in Yale Romanization), ed. Kwan Choi Wah, Lo Chi Hung, Lo Tam Fee Yin, Mak Tze Kuen, Man Chiu Kwan, Miu Wong Nga Ching, Pauline Ng Shiu King, New Asia Yale-in-China Chinese Language Centre, The Chinese University of Hong Kong, 1994.

Putonghua *Concise English-Chinese Chinese-English Dictionary,* The Commercial Press/Oxford University Press, Beijing/Hong Kong, 1986

MUSICAL REFERENCES:

Christmas (1969) "See me, feel me, touch me, heal me" from The Who's rock opera *Tommy* composed by Pete Townshend and John Entwistle

Darn That Dream (1939) Music by Jimmy Van Heusen and Lyrics by Eddie de Lange; introduced in *Swingin' The Dream* (1939)

Good Morning (1939) from *Babes in Arms,* Music and Lyrics by Arthur Freed and Nacio Herb Brown

Heart & Soul (1938) Music by Hoagy Carmichael and Lyrics by Frank Loesser

House of Bamboo (1958) Music and Lyrics by Bill Crompton and Norman Murrells; version referenced recorded by Earl Grant (1960)

La Donna È Mobile **(1851)** from the opera *Rigoletto* by Verdi

Misty (1954) Music by Erroll Garner and Lyrics by Johnny Burke

Moonglow (1934) Music and Lyrics by Will Hudson / Edgar DeLange / Irving Mills

Stardust (1929) Music by Hoagy Carmichael and Lyrics by Mitchell Parish

The Glory of Love (1939) Music and Lyrics by William Hill

Voulez-vous coucher avec moi (ce soir) **Lady Marmalade (1975)** Music and Lyrics by Bob Crewe and Kenny Nolan